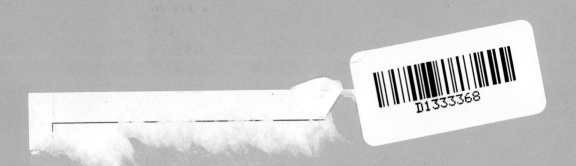

ARE YOU WEARING
SOFT SOLED SHOES
NO PROPERTIES, MUSICAL INSTRUMENTS
OR TECHNICAL EQUIPMENT MUST BE
HANDLED, OR FURNITURE SAT ON
EXCEPT IN THE COURSE OF DUTY

PRODUCTION   INSIDE BBC
TELEVISION

INSIDE BBC TELEVISION

A Year Behind the Camera

Introduction by Richard Baker

Webb & Bower

BBC TV

First published in Great Britain 1983 by
Webb & Bower (Publishers) Limited
9 Colleton Crescent, Exeter, Devon EX2 4BY
in collaboration with BBC TV,
BBC Television Centre, Wood Lane,
London W12 7RJ

Text: Rosalie Horner
Photographs: John Timbers
Editor: Ruth Rosenthal
Designer: Paul Watkins

Copyright © Webb & Bower (Publishers)
Limited/BBC TV 1983

British Library Cataloguing in Publication Data
Inside BBC television
 1. British Broadcasting Corporation—Pictorial
works
 2. Television—Great Britain—Production
and direction—Political works
 I. Rosenthal, Ruth   II. Horner, Rosalie
III. Baker, Richard, *1925*
791.45′022   PN1992.3.G7

ISBN 0–906671–77–9

Typeset in Great Britain by August Filmsetting,
Warrington WA2 7AF

Printed and bound in Italy by
New Interlitho SpA

Picture credits:

All photographs by John Timbers with the exception of the following:
BBC Enterprises 68–73; BBC PA 36 (bottom left); BBC Picture Public-
ity 32 (top), 33, 34 (top), 35; BBC TV News 36 (others); BBC Topical
Programme Unit 141–5; Chris Capstick 176–7; David Clarke David
Edwards 212–16; Jim Clay 54; Colorsport 14 (top); Michael Cullen
178–9; David Edwards 108–111; Conrad Hafenrichter 6; Mark Jen-
kinson 149; Ned Kelly 152 (bottom) 153, 155, 156; Peter Lane 190–91;
Press Association 32 (bottom); Diana Richards 152 (top); Michael
Sanders 170–75; Syndication International 34 (bottom); Adrian Warren
150, 151, 154 (left); Joan Williams 132, 133

Artwork: Trevor Goring, Peter Jones 99–101

Cartoon: Gerald Scarfe 11

Previous pages: BBC Television Centre, London, at dusk.

Contents

Foreword
Aubrey Singer

The year covered by this book has been a memorable one for the BBC television service. *Breakfast Time* was planned and launched, and it has amply rewarded the confidence we had in it from the beginning by outstripping its rival both in terms of audience and of critical acclaim.

Those of us who have the good fortune to work in television are inclined to look on all the marvels of our electronic world as nothing more than the tools of our trade, which indeed they are. But from time to time we catch the excitement—the awe, even—engendered in people who enter Television Centre for the first time. There are thousands of them every year, but there are still more thousands who would like to visit us and who cannot do so for various reasons, one of which is that we are usually extremely busy making programmes!

I hope that this book will prove a source of pleasure and information to those people, and that it will stimulate the interest of others in the work of BBC Television. The original idea came from Richard Cawston and Michael Bunce. Nothing like it has ever been published before: we have never submitted ourselves to such a searching examination by camera. Looking at the resulting pictures, we realise that what to us are the nuts and bolts of our trade—the studio, the scanner, the camera stand, the gallery—have a special beauty of their own. I am delighted to be able to share it with you.

Aubrey Singer Managing Director BBC Television

Introduction

Richard Baker

This book is a celebration of BBC Television fifty years on from the start of experimental transmissions by the BBC in 1932, and it is a subject worth celebrating. I have worked for the outfit for over thirty years and hope to continue as long as they'll let me, so I'm hardly likely to knock the product; but you don't have to take my word for it. 'The BBC is arguably the single most important cultural organisation in the nation', the Annan Report had to say, before uttering a word of adverse criticism; 'it has over many years raised the level of taste and discrimination'. Far from being what Milton Schulman called in 1973 'the Least Worst Television in the World', the BBC Television Service is still regarded internationally as one of the world's best. The pictures and stories you will find in these pages help to explain why.

When I first joined the BBC in 1950, Television was a small outpost of the BBC empire, inhabited, some thought, by irresponsible lunatics rightly confined to the ghetto of Alexandra Palace on the remote heights of North London. There, in 1936, in two tiny studios, the BBC had put on the air the world's first high-definition television service, and it was from there that most TV programmes still originated. The BBC had just acquired—in November 1949—the Rank film studios at Lime Grove in Shepherds Bush, and the TV people were pushing hard for more money, more facilities. But there was still scepticism in influential quarters about the future of television. One of the most determined pioneers of the BBC Television Service, Grace Wyndham Goldie, was told by the philosopher, Bertrand Russell, that the medium 'will be of no importance in your lifetime or mine'. Radio was still the big thing in home entertainment. By the end of 1950, only about a million people had access to television; the really big audiences were drawn by radio successes like *Ray's a Laugh*, *Take it from Here* and *Have a Go*, and the main news programmes on Radio 4's predecessor, the Home Service, attracted the kind of attention now given to the *Nine O'Clock News* on BBC1.

What a revolution has taken place in the last thirty years inside the BBC; a bloodless revolution, though the battles for control between Television and Radio have often been hard and bitter in the past, and there are times even now when the rival claims of these two great strands of the BBC's output can ruffle the truce between them. BBC mandarins are used to commuting between the Television Centre, next door to White City stadium in West London, and Broadcasting House in the heart of the West End, but television's managers are not altogether sorry to be separated by a few miles from what they are apt to refer to as 'the Oxford Circus branch'. 'BH' is still the BBC's headquarters, and it is there that the Board of Governors most often meet, though the Director-General, Alasdair Milne, like the Chairman, also has a sixth-floor office at the Television Centre and is very often to be seen in it.

BBC Television's Managing Director, Aubrey Singer, inhabits the office next door. He has at his disposal some sixty per cent of the BBC's total budget which amounted in the year 1981-2 to 605 million pounds. That means about a million pounds a day was spent on the Television Service, including what it costs to transmit and distribute programmes, and to maintain regional television as well as the two main networks. Aubrey Singer and BBC Television are in business in a very big way.

BBC TV belongs to the people

They are not in business to make money, though an important, if relatively small, profit is made through the sale of programmes and from publications. They are in business to provide a public service paid for by public subscription, through a licence fee which is one of the lowest in Europe for colour TV and absolutely the lowest for black and white. In a very special way, BBC TV belongs to the people. A commercial network aims to bring in customers of course, but the people they have to please first and foremost are their commercial masters and above all the advertisers. It is they who call the tune, as we have been reminded in recent times with the troubles of TV-am and Channel Four.

Of course the self-interest of commercial broadcasters can often be remarkably enlightened: the BBC has no monopoly of good programmes. But in spite of all the pressure now put on the Corporation by commercial interests, it still strives to adhere to an essentially different philosophy. As the BBC said in its evidence to the Annan Committee, 'popular entertainment, sport, drama, music can all be nudged in the direction of serving some other interest than that for which they were created. No BBC programme should ever have an ulterior motive. In this sense, truth to the word and image is at the heart of public service broadcasting.' An admirable posture, if increasingly hard to maintain in these days of commercial sponsorship of almost every major event.

A question of accountability

Essentially it's a question of accountability. If you don't evade paying your TV licence, it's *your* money the BBC uses to provide you with Television—and Radio—programmes (minus seven per cent deducted by British Telecom for their costs in collecting the licence money and tracking down back-sliders), and if you don't like what you are getting, you have the clearest of rights to say so. It is, in a quite literal sense, *your* BBC. Or rather it's ours, because BBC employees are not excused from buying a licence and feel at least as deeply as anyone else about the content of the service. Indeed we have a proprietary interest which makes us care a great deal

about what you think of us, and we react with sharp concern if we get badly beaten by the Opposition.

The presence of rivals in the field since ITV went on the air in 1956 has unquestionably acted as a stimulus to the BBC. A certain monolithic smugness used to hang in the air when I first joined the Corporation. That, and a paternalistic certainty that the BBC knew what was best for its customers. The sense of responsibility remains, but there's no reason to feel smug.

TV is a high-risk business

ITV at the time of writing gets about fifty per cent of the available audience taking the year as a whole. Aubrey Singer regards this broadly equal division of the market between the commercial and public service product as 'an unwritten rule of British TV': it does, after all, represent a considerable redressing of the balance of earlier days when ITV commanded seventy-five per cent of the audience. The BBC has to battle for its share, though Singer claims he is not so much concerned with figures as 'the feel of the shows'. He won't 'go downmarket' to capture the vast public which consistently watches *Crossroads*; he doesn't see that as the BBC's job. He's in the business, as he puts it, of 'husbandry'—nurturing the talent, wit and skill of his large team to produce the best possible programmes. He regards people as by far his most important resource—discovering talent, building it up, and trusting it to produce the goods. But television is 'a high risk business' and you can never be sure you've got it right. Whoever would have imagined that three old men living lives of amiable futility in a Yorkshire village would provide material for a long-running favourite comedy series? *Last of the Summer Wine* now consistently well up in the top twenty, was a slow starter when it first went on the air over a decade ago, but the BBC, believing that the 'feel of the show' was right, stayed with it, and this faith paid of. Having taken the initial risk, it then becomes a question of nerve, if you think you have a winner and the public at first doesn't agree. New ideas in comedy are particularly vulnerable in the early stages—even *MASH* had poor ratings when it first went on the air.

Perhaps the most extraordinary comedy success of 1982 was *Yes Minister*—and not only of 1982. It first went on the air in February 1980, and since then there have been two further series; each of them has won the BAFTA best comedy award, making *Yes Minister* a record-breaker in that it is the first comedy series ever to win this award three years running.

I suppose most of us cherish a secret suspicion that the way our system of government functions is farcical, but it took a remarkable combination of insight, courage and wit to say so in public for weeks on end and get away with it. Fortunately for the cause of comedy, though he would hardly have seen his work at the time in that light,

Anthony Jay had been producing politicians in current affairs programmes since 1955 and had acquired a considerable knowledge of the way they went about things. When he was setting up the interviews between Sir Harold Wilson and David Frost, it suddenly dawned on him that the relationship between the Permanent Secretary and his Cabinet Minister was the key to the way 'our modern so-called democracy' (Jay's words) really worked. It became clear that the way things happened, or rather didn't happen, was due to the inevitable tension between civil servants and politicians, who are nevertheless bound together by their need for each other. In the middle, striving to hold the balance, is that desperately anxious figure, the Private Secretary.

For a time, Jay kept to himself the conviction that all this had enormous comic potential with, at the heart of it, a great deal of human interest. Then he shared the idea with Jonathan Lynn, who at once saw the opportunities it afforded, to examine the processes of government decision-making in a comedy formula which could illuminate as well as entertain.

Jay and Lynn took the first script to the BBC in 1977, but although the Head of Comedy was very keen, it was thought best to wait until after the General Election. Three years elapsed before *Yes Minister* was screened.

It was a success from the first. The casting was perfect, the situations convincing though it took some time to make the audience realise that the story lines were in fact authentic: there is nothing half so unbelievable as the truth. Before long, real cabinet ministers were admitting that the series was hideously faithful to the way things happen in Whitehall, and *Yes Minister* was on the map not just as a comedy series but as a sharply observed comment on the way we are governed.

Since the advent of BBC2, the BBC has taken full advantage of the opportunity for experiment offered by an alternative channel. Controller, BBC2 has become the great commissioner of new ideas—ideas often taken over, once they have been developed, by BBC1. On its own two channels, the BBC is able to offer a balanced choice of viewing to the public. But as between BBC and ITV, overall balance can suffer, in my opinion, in the cause of the ratings battle. That is one of the prices paid for competition. The pitting of like against like—the simultaneous transmission of massive sports coverage on Saturday afternoon, the timing of *Omnibus* against the *South Bank Show* on Sunday nights, are just two examples of the way competition can operate against the public interest, though it no doubt helps the sale of video recorders and certainly stimulates each side to try to outdo the opposition. But there are some areas where competition has without question resulted in a better service to the public. News is a case in point. No newsman ever likes to be beaten on a good story, and in the field of television news the rivalry between the ITN and BBC teams is a very real factor in their lives. Each side wants to produce the quickest—and best—account of any given story, two qualities which are by no means always compatible in journalism. Our news programmes are no doubt monitored with vigilance at ITN; we certainly view their output with close attention in our newsroom. 'ITN had it, why didn't we?' is a question no Duty Editor likes to be asked.

Who watches what

Whether for the sake of establishing the size of the audience or what people think about our programmes, it is very important for the BBC to know as far as possible who watches what.

The Corporation has been in the business of audience measurement since 1939, and until recently based its conclusions entirely on daily interviews with a sample of the population. In 1980, ITV and BBC joined forces to set up the Broadcasters' Audience Research Board (BARB) and agreed to abide by its findings. Now an estimate of the number of viewers watching any given programme is reached through the operation of meters fitted to television sets in about 2900 private households. In addition, the 8000 or so individuals over the age of four, who comprise those households, and their visitors, are asked to keep detailed diaries of their TV viewing. The households concerned are chosen to reflect the social balance of the country as a whole, and it is from the records they yield that an estimated total number of viewers is arrived at. Apart from the numbers game, however, the sample yields a lot of other valuable information about viewing habits.

A never-ending dilemma

Planners and producers need to know the quality of appreciation as well as the mere size of the audience. How much did people enjoy this or that programme, and why? To get this information, the BBC's Broadcasting Research Department, acting as agents for BARB, question a representative sample of 1000 people over the age of 12 every day, and ask them to fill in a small booklet called 'What do you think of what you watch?' over the following five days. From these enquiries, an Appreciation Index is built up. People are asked to rate a given programme on a six point scale ranging from 1—not at all interesting and/or enjoyable—to 6—extremely interesting and/or enjoyable; and from these ratings, an 'AI' figure ranging from 1–100 is produced which gives a fair indication of how far the programme has achieved its objectives. Total numbers may be very large or relatively small, but that will not be the only factor affecting the continuation of a certain strand of programmes; also very important will be the value of what is produced, and its place in the balance of the output as a whole. The decision as to what to broadcast and when, in a BBC which is no longer a monopoly, is compounded by the need to command a mass audience while continuing to satisfy the innumerable minorities which make up that mass. Maintaining the right balance places the BBC in a never-ending dilemma.

* * *

The immense variety of BBC Television programmes will be apparent in the pages that follow. Between them they enable the BBC to fill a role in society which would have been inconceivable a generation ago.

As a purveyor of news, it commands a public larger than the most successful newspaper; it is a theatre or cinema capable of seating in home comfort the entire population of the British Isles; it is school and university for millions of students; concert hall and opera house for the music lover, football stadium and cricket field, racecourse, art gallery, church. Through television, the scientist shares the result of his research, the explorer takes us on his expeditions, the politician struggles to preserve his public image. Sportsmen and surgeons, industrial leaders, everyday people and Royal personages, all express themselves through the medium of television, which is the most cohesive force in modern society as well as the most dangerous, in that, used uncritically, it can swamp the individual and relieve him of the need to think for himself. No one would deny that television is a power in the land or that BBC Television has a unique importance in the broadcasting spectrum.

Unique, but how secure? 1982 brought the report of the Hunt Committee on cable television and the ensuing debate in and out of Parliament. The BBC expressed itself in favour of cable television in general, but was eager that the safeguards against unscrupulous exploitation should be made effective. The BBC's fear is that network television, and thus the great majority of viewers, could be deprived of popular programme material. It's been estimated that at most fifty to sixty per cent of the country could be economically provided with access to cable, and even where it was available, many people would be unable to afford to buy into the system. Thus there would come about class divisions in mass communication of a kind which has always been anathema to the BBC. Moreover there would also be a tendency to import more ready-made programmes from abroad, most notably from America, thus hastening what one BBC chief calls 'the Canadianisation' of Great Britain—the drowning of indigenous talent in a tidal wave of entertainment from a too-powerful neighbour. There is also the likelihood that the viewing audience will become even more fragmented than it is at present—a gain in terms of individual choice for a few, at the expense of a medium of information and entertainment which has hitherto been shared by all.

The capacity of the BBC to bring the nation together stems from a history which dates back more than sixty years. Its reputation for authority and impartiality in matters of news and current affairs, shaken from time to time but not shattered, comes from the early days under John Reith, who stood up to pressure from Whitehall as far back as the General Strike of 1926 and helped to ensure that the BBC never became the Government broadcasting service.

A purveyor of truth

Part of the BBC legend arises from its role in the Second World War as a purveyor of truth, no matter how disagreeable that truth might be; and in times of crisis and celebration alike, the nation still seems to look to the BBC for the full authoritative account. Thus with our reporting of the Falklands crisis of 1982, as with many a national event in the past, the BBC's share of the television audience increased dramatically.

In the case of the Falklands story, especially in its early stages when material was more readily available from the South American mainland than from the Task Force, the BBC's decision to present both sides of the case came in for violent criticism. When Richard Francis, Managing Director of BBC Radio, declared at a conference in Spain that 'the widow of Portsmouth is no different from the widow of Buenos Aires', he was expressing a sentiment which was at once professional and humane; yet the phrase, given wide publicity, profoundly shocked the British public who virtually overnight had become almost unanimously partisan. Francis was only reiterating a time-honoured creed when he said that the BBC's reputation 'did not come from being tied to the British Government's apron strings, nor from banging a drum for the British Task Force' and he quite correctly concluded that 'the BBC needs no lesson in patriotism'. Fortunately as time went on and it became possible to show more pictures of our own operations to back up some magnificent reporting, criticism of our coverage largely evaporated; although as it subsided, it left behind many questions. Perhaps as a result of these questions there will be a fundamental reappraisal of the attitude of the military to the media in time of armed conflict, and some reflection on the appropriate role of a public broadcasting service when the nation is at war. How, in the 1980s and beyond, is patriotism to be reconciled with truth?

I read the news on BBC TV for more than a quarter of a century, and I never felt more emotionally involved than during the Falklands crisis. It was partly I suppose that I have been connected with the Royal Navy for much of my life both during the Second World War and subsequently as a member of the Royal Naval Reserve, and I knew personally a number of people in the Task Force; but I was also aware in a particularly acute way, of the involvement of the public in what was happening—of their hunger for news and their fear of bad news. In television, to some extent, we work in an enclosed world bounded by the studio, the cameras and the lights, and are apt to become obsessed with the technical problems of getting a programme on the air. It is necessary to be reminded from time to time of the closeness of the audience, and during the Falklands period we had a sharp reminder. I'd experienced this sense of two-way communication with an unseen audience before, most memorably during our reporting of the Aberfan pit disaster of 1966 in which 116 children died. The details of that tragedy became progressively more appalling during the course of a single lunchtime news bulletin—terrible enough for those who were not directly concerned, and unthinkable in their impact for parents and relatives who were learning the news from us. The most important thing for any broadcaster to remember is that he is talking to individual people with personal feelings, even though those individuals may add up in aggregate to an audience of millions.

* * *

The moment of communication on the screen in any programme comes at the end of a long and complex process involving many different skills. In news for instance, there is the reporter, the cameraman and sound recordist who rush off to cover a story in the field, using either traditional film or Electronic News Gathering (ENG) equipment—small portable TV cameras and video recorders. Pictures must be got back to base, and edited. Meanwhile, the word merchants in the newsroom prepare script material, caption artists work on maps and other illustrative material, the production team decides how to present the story in the studio. I once worked out that seventy people could easily be involved in putting a news story on the screen, ranging from the Editor and studio director in the production gallery, through studio managers, sound and vision technicians, film and videotape operators to the motorbike messenger who'd brought material through the rush-hour streets. And that's only one part of one kind of programme. Whatever kind of television you're talking about, for every person who appears on the screen, there could well be twenty others just as indispensable to the operation who are never seen.

Sometimes in the intervals between news programmes, I would take a visitor round the Television Centre, and I never ceased to be amazed by what I saw. A television

11

studio gallery in operation is always an absorbing sight. The director, flanked on one side by his assistant with stop-watch in hand and on the other by his 'vision mixer', sits in front of an array of TV screens which show him the many ingredients of the programme he is making. The output of the cameras in the studio itself, of film or videotape machines loaded with material to be fed into the programme on cue, of outside broadcast cameras perhaps, is displayed before the director, who has to decide how and when to use it. He may have on the desk, as in drama, a script which has been prepared to the last detail in advance, or, as in news and current affairs, it may be a question of 'busking' with the best information available to him as a story develops. It's a job that requires concentration and quick thinking to a very high degree.

Acting – a disciplined business

Or come into a drama studio and watch the actors at work. After rehearsing for days or perhaps weeks in an outside studio, often enough a church hall, using make-shift furniture and props and with the set marked out with chalk lines, they come into the studio itself for a day or two and must bring the play to life. Everything, it seems to me, is against them. They work in tiny sets, watching every move to the inch, with cameras and lights and microphones often only a few inches from their faces, and under these circumstances they not only have to remember their lines, but create a character and make us believe in it. Sometimes a play will be recorded more or less in the order in which it was written, but often enough scenes are recorded out of sequence, as in films. The actor must be able to hit off the precise feeling required, not just once but often several times, for reasons which may have nothing to do with his performance, but are concerned with technical problems of one kind and another. Acting of any sort is a disciplined business, but television acting seems to me the most demanding of all.

Performing in other types of programmes creates other kinds of problems. It may be that sometimes you have the help of an Autocue machine—a device that displays the words you want across the lens of the camera you are looking at. This can be of great assistance in looking directly at your audience, but it needs practice. We have all seen the inexperienced presenter who is so riveted to the Autocue that he cannot take his eyes off it for a single second. But there are many occasions when Autocue cannot be used. Then the presenter needs a good instant memory and the capacity to think of several things at once: the facts he has to convey, the guest he has to interview, what is going to happen next, what the studio director is saying to him in his earpiece, and the hieroglyphic signs being made to him by the floor manager. All this while looking perfectly natural and unperturbed. Among masters of this game, none is more

adept than Frank Bough, whose apparently unshakeable ease has set the tone of the BBC's extraordinarily successful breakfast programme, which was being planned at the end of 1982.

* * *

Breakfast Time comes from the Lime Grove studios in Shepherd's Bush, just a few hundred yards down the road from the Television Centre. These, with the addition of the Television Theatre and the Greenwood Theatre, are the main studio facilities in London. Another vastly important programme-making centre is at Ealing film studios. Here, British films have been made since as long ago as 1907, and they still are—by the BBC. BBC film crews operate around the clock all round the world and between them they account for some fifteen hours of new programme material for network television every week.

But London is by no means the only programme-making centre in the BBC. There are network production centres at Manchester, Birmingham and Bristol, where the natural history unit is based, and major national centres for Scotland, Wales and Northern Ireland at Glasgow, Cardiff and Belfast respectively, as well as a number of other smaller English Regional centres. All make their own programmes for their own audience and contribute in a greater or lesser degree to the national networks.

Of the many different types of programmes to be seen on BBC TV, sport fills the largest amount of screen times— twenty-seven per cent in 1981. Sport is popular; it is also relatively cheap to put on the air. At £20,000 per hour, it is the most economical strand in our output, except for programmes bought in from outside—films and the like—which average out at £12,000 per hour. At the other end of the scale, light entertainment is quite expensive at £72,000 per hour, but by far the most costly ingredient is drama, which comes out at £170,000 per hour, and it accounts for six per cent of the total output of BBC TV. Expensive or not, drama—and that includes serials as well as one-off plays—is one of the more prestigious of the BBC's activities and accounts for a high proportion of programme sales overseas.

In the early days, plays, like everything else on television, were put out 'live', and there are those who think this is still the best way to televise drama. For the most part, plays and serials are recorded on videotape, a process which allows for re-takes if necessary and will ultimately produce a more polished and considered result. The drama—or documentary—you see on your screen is an intricate cocktail of many ingredients. It may consist of scenes performed in a studio with others filmed on location elsewhere, mixed with captions, maps, still photographs and recorded background music or effects. The performer who appears on screen is only one small part of the total mix, whose ultimate flavour is the creation of the producer working for long hours with his film or videotape editor. If the work is well done, the final carefully wrought artefact will appear spontaneous and uncontrived.

That is one kind of television. There is another, and to me it is the truest kind. The very word means 'seeing things which are far distant from us', and when to that concept is added the ability to see events as they occur, then the magic of television is at its most potent. There is a particular excitement in working on a live outside broadcast, whether of the *Last Night of the Proms*, a ceremonial occasion, the *Grand National*, golf, soccer, darts or snooker. However well prepared you are, however much research you have done, however much you know about the matter in hand, there is always the possibility of the totally unexpected happening, and this makes the adrenalin flow fiercely in all those involved — cameraman, director, sound engineer, commentator.

For the viewer too, this is a specially riveting kind of television. Who will forget, in 1982, the emotive drama of the fleet leaving Portsmouth for the South Atlantic, and the triumphant return of the ships after battle? Or the visit to Britain of the Pope against the tense background of the Falklands campaign? The coverage of those eventful days, shared for once between BBC and ITV, was utterly compelling television, all the more so because of the conflicting feelings generated by the situation.

Here in these pages you will gain an impression of how BBC Television sets about performing in a single year the many different roles it is now called upon to play in our national life. There is a great fascination for us all in looking behind the scenes of someone else's profession, no matter what it is. Where television is concerned, it is rather like finding out how the conjuror performs his magic. But if the trick is a good one, even when you know how it's done, it will not lose its power to baffle and amaze you. Such is the case with *Beau Geste*, the making of which involved any amount of elaborate trickery on the sand dunes of Dorset, much of it revealed in this book. But somehow when we see the finished product we are still transported, as the producer intends us to be, to a desert fort in North Africa occupied by the desperadoes of the French Foreign Legion.

*   *   *

Truth is what all good television is about, though the way it's told can sometimes appear like the strangest fiction.

Horses going over the dramatic Bechers Brook and (*below*) a crew recording dawn gallops.

The Grand National

Fred Viner, one of the three producers who cover the race, in his outside broadcast scanner.

The Grand National, that spectacular four-mile race which covers 30 hair-raising jumps in 10 minutes, makes great demands on the resources of television and its three senior producers Fred Viner, Richard Tilling and Nick Hunter.

In the case of the Aintree National, the major race of the three-day meeting, there are extra pressures because its fame commands a potential worldwide audience of 300 million. Even those who hardly know one end of a horse from another have heard of the National.

'You get a real prickle of apprehension at the back of your neck,' says Hunter who looks after the five cameras in the 'country' unit. This covers the breathtaking Bechers, (one of racing's most dangerous jumps, with a camera mounted above the ditch and one below it), the Canal Turn and four other fences.

'Unlike Fred and Rickie who have been covering the other races, the only time I see any horses on my cameras is the Grand National,' he says. 'I've been sitting there for two or three hours which is a long time to think about what might go wrong. It's a nerve-racking race to cover. It's one race and if a mistake is made on a fence like Bechers a lot of people will be speaking to me.'

Veteran sports producer Fred Viner controls 11 cameras which film the start and finish of the race. He is responsible for the overall coverage and switches between his own and Nick Hunter's cameras.

Richard Tilling is in the linking scanner—the mobile control room. This has six cameras which concentrate on everything that is not on the actual race-course; the paddock, the horses leaving the parade ring, entering the unsaddling enclosure and all the interviews.

This notoriously dangerous race which has achieved a glamour not even the Derby can rival, abounds in legends. What other horse-race could produce a champion as valiant and big-hearted as three-times winner Red Rum? And of course Enid Bagnold's classic *National Velvet* about a girl who disguises herself as a lad to enter and win the race came one step closer to fact in 1977 when women jockeys were admitted, and in 1982 when Geraldine Rees on Cheers became the first girl to finish.

As a result the world and his wife—from Prince Charles down—want to see the race.

'Every horse had been backed by somebody and everybody wants to see what happens to his horse. At the same time it is the biggest and hardest race and we are trying to get that over,' says Hunter. 'So there is always a battle in your mind between trying to give a big close-up and trying to stand back for the long shot.'

'The nightmare is where one horse is one fence ahead of everyone else,' he continues. 'Naturally you want to see the leader but you also want to see the rest of the field, as well as showing them both in relation to each other.'

Twenty cameras are needed to cover the event, most of which are set on 30-foot-high rostra around the course. There are also a couple of lightweight cameras and another mounted on a car known as a CRE (Colour Roving Eye) which runs parallel to the race.

Prince Charles and The Princess of Wales often watch the end of the race from Hunter's 'country' scanner. In 1982 Viner called through on his intercom to ask if the Royals had gone. 'It was a bit difficult for me to say "No, they are standing right beside me".'

15

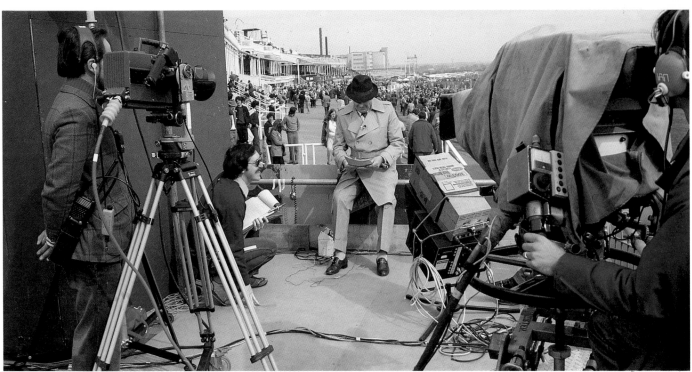

David Coleman putting the finishing touches to his script before the start of the Grand National.
Below: Cameraman covering the finish of the race above the main grandstand.

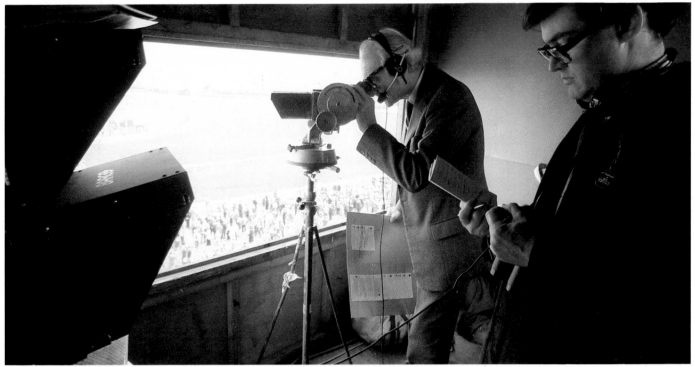

Peter O'Sullevan covering the race from his commentary box and (*below*) commentator Julian Wilson climbing up one of the twelve 30-ft-high scaffolding towers to the television commentary box (directly above the radio position).

17

The colour roving eye (CRE) with a camera mounted on top of the car which travels alongside the race at speeds of up to 40 mph.

Cameraman (*above*) and engineer controlling the television picture from the CRE.

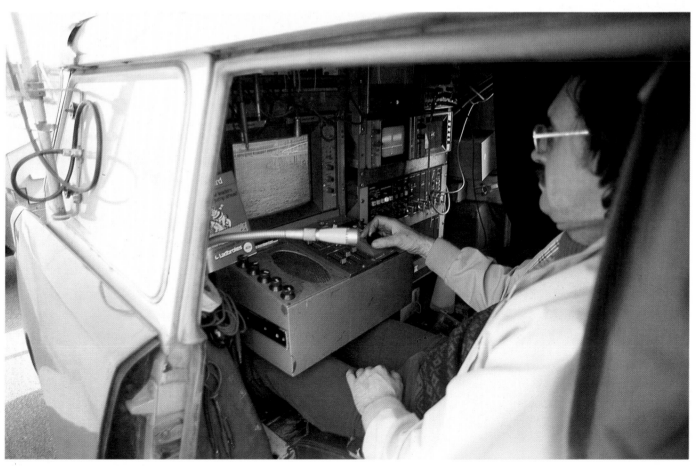

Overleaf: David Coleman interviewing the 1982 Grand National winner, amateur jockey Dick Saunders. On the left is jockey Geraldine Rees, the first girl to finish the race.

'It's a bit like boxing with one hand tied behind you,' says Michael Hurll, executive producer and director, who was in charge of his second Eurovision contest in 1982. 'You try to give the show some production value because you can't do anything about the content. You try and dress it up and make it palatable but you can't have sensational lighting for one number because it would seem unfair to the others. All the acts have to look equal without being equally boring.'

In the interests of fairness, Hurll had designer Graeme Storey and his assistant Peter Higgins create an all-purpose set, capable of being converted in 18 different ways. It must complement the acts, not dominate them.

The Eurovision Song Contest is an unusual occasion for, unlike every other event in this book, no one at the BBC has actually chosen to produce it. It is an inherited, if somewhat burdensome, honour given to the country that produced the previous year's winner. The number one success of Buck's Fizz in 1981 meant that Britain, and in particular, the Harrogate Conference Centre, was host in 1982 to the 27th Eurovision Song Contest and the 17 other participating countries.

'You always come away from Eurovision feeling you have achieved the result required but you wouldn't put it down as your most creative work in the world of television,' says Hurll. 'Your contribution is mainly organisational, getting together a big technical operation.'

Eurovision is an important international public relations exercise and goes out to 30 countries with an audience of 300 million. Apart from the production team of 35 technicians and 4 camera crews, it also commands the presence of a dozen BBC executives, known as the Operations Group, who include the Heads of Light Entertainment and Variety, as well as three people from the European Broadcasting Union and seven personnel from the Conference Centre.

'One of the big problems is security,' Hurll continues, 'when dealing with 18 countries, every one of which seems to have some subversive group working within it whom it would suit to create a diversion during the live transmission.' Harrogate bristled with security. In charge was Derek Butcher of the BBC's Central Services Division who worked with the Chief Constable of North Yorkshire and the Chief Superintendent of Harrogate, with various members of the Special Branch in evidence as well.

Metal detectors checked each of the thousand people involved in the Festival, their bags and photographic equipment. When an escalator set one of these devices off, comfort was sacrificed in the interests of security. The moving staircase was turned off and people had to walk up the equivalent of three floors to reach the hall.

Security is so strict that even being Director-General of the BBC will not gain you entry if you do not have the right pass. This happened some years ago to Sir Charles Curran when he was Director-General. He was made to wait outside the barrier while a suitable identity card was made up for him. 'We guarantee a mouse can't get into the place,' says Geoff Jowitt, a production manager.

Before a large percentage of the civilised world was allowed to sample the delights of Portugal's 'Bem-Bom', the opening song, 24 security guards, 6 uniformed BBC commissionaires and a clutch of police dogs made a thorough search of the Harrogate Centre. They had to make sure that the only boom bang-a-bang to be heard during the evening would be in the lyrics.

22

Eurovision Song Contest

Announcer Jan Leeming rehearsing in the 2000-seat Harrogate Conference Centre the day before *Eurovision* 1982.

Set designer Graeme Storey (right) and his assistant Peter Higgins with the working model
in front of the set in the early stages of construction, and (*centre*) a week later.

The main camera, the Tulip crane (left), used for mid-shots onstage.

OB scanners arrived a week early for the technical crew to rig the cable network.

Contestants from the 18 competing countries backstage during final dress rehearsal.

Omnibus: Leonard Bernstein

'It seemed the ideal combination,' says Humphrey Burton (producer of Music and Arts programmes), 'one of the world's leading symphony orchestras and one of the world's leading conductors.'

Leonard Bernstein was invited by Robert Ponsonby, Controller of Music, BBC Radio to conduct Elgar's *Enigma Variations*. Ponsonby suggested to Burton that he might like to televise the event live from the Festival Hall in conjunction with Radio 3. Subsequently an *Omnibus* documentary of the studio rehearsals was also planned.

'Bernstein has always admired Elgar's use of word play and he shares his love of word puzzles,' continues Burton.

However, the combination got off to a less than ideal start when Bernstein arrived 25 minutes late for the first of five rehearsals and soon revealed that he had some variations of his own for Elgar's work which, to put it mildly, were considered a trifle eccentric by the musicians.

Bernstein wanted it to be played very slowly.

'Some of the orchestra were surprised, others were very upset and considered it to be a gross distortion,' continues Burton. 'In the "Nimrod", for example, he went twice as slowly as it had been played before and it sounded absolutely marvellous.'

A further source of discord between the flamboyant American maestro and the orchestra was his constant chat. 'Many of the orchestra thought he talked too much,' says Burton. Especially one of the trumpeters who got the sharp edge of the Bernstein tongue and in the documentary is seen blushing as a result. But such reactions are the very life-blood of a documentary and to capture these a producer must rely heavily on his vision mixer, in this case Angela Wilson.

'You need a very, very alert vision mixer to choose which camera to look at at any given moment so it becomes a collaboration between the two of you, sometimes working in an improvised way,' Burton says. And to record the musicians' verbal responses, a series of extra microphones, similar to those used in Sir Robin Day's *Question Time* was installed to pick up the talk-back.

For sound supervisor Anthony Philpot, the recording was very different from the usual way of working. 'Normally when recording a symphony orchestra for broadcast you have them play for 15 minues in order to adjust the mike position and balance the sound,' he says. 'But my brief stated no sound rehearsal with the orchestra because Humphrey particularly wanted to capture the moment Bernstein approached the orchestra and started rehearsing. It was very revealing. He talked for 90 minutes before they played a note.'

'Part of a conductor's work is to impose his personality on a piece,' says Burton. 'Bernstein is a past master of the orchestra so even though these very busy, intense rehearsals started with the musicians resenting him, they ended up thinking his view valid.'

'My job for *Omnibus* was to reflect the ups and downs of the rehearsals,' says Burton, 'and also to let the audience see the music growing and developing under Bernstein's hand. We showed this in 3 of the 13 *Variations*.'

'Every possible eventuality was covered so that even when he went into his dressing-room he was wired up and a camera went in with him.' This close observation of the conductor at work is something which Bernstein revels in says Burton, who has worked with him often over the last 20 years. 'He has a great sense of history and of his own destiny,' says Burton. 'He knows the useful nature of this kind of exercise and that's why he will co-operate with you.'

BBC **Symphony Orchestra cello and double-bass cases.**

Producer Humphrey Burton giving rehearsal notes to the orchestra in Studio One.

Leonard Bernstein being interviewed by Barry Norman for the *Omnibus* programme.

Overleaf: The recording session.

Orchestral rehearsal with 1982 finalist, horn player Jeanette Murphy, in BBC North's music studio.

Young Musician of the Year

Piano finalists with producer Helen Morton (left) before the winner is announced.

Anna Markland, before she won the competition, at the final rehearsal with the BBC Northern Symphony Orchestra.

'*Young Musician* is not a competition that will lead to stardom,' says the producer, Roy Tipping. 'It is meant to be a showcase for British youth music. However much fame the winner gets as a result, he or she is still a long way from being a full professional.'

'The reason we chose under 19 as the age limit for entry was because it excluded anyone who was getting full-time college tuition,' he says. 'We didn't want it to be regarded as one of the ways into the profession because there are plenty of other competitions which already do this.'

Young Musician of the Year started in 1978 and is held every second year. In 1982, there were 700 entrants and each one was heard over a period of three months. Tipping hears about a third of them and six regional producers listen to the rest.

Out of that number, 200 go forward. A fortnight is set aside when they play in one of the five different centres around the country. From their number, 44 semi-finalists emerge. They are divided equally among the four instrumental groups of piano, strings, wind and brass. Eleven are chosen in each group because it was felt that that was the maximum number which could be handled conveniently in one day's adjudication, given that each competitor performed for 25 minutes with five minutes of interview.

By the time these 44 are known, it becomes a gruelling countdown to transmission for Tipping, the presenter, Humphrey Burton, and everyone connected with the production.

'We record eight days on the run, out of which come seven programmes,' says Tipping. 'It's a most exhausting time. On one famous occasion I went to sleep leaning against a wall!'

Tipping's day begins at 9 am in the Concert Hall of the

Royal Northern College of Music in Manchester. It ends around 2 am the next day. Lunch is the time when Tipping, Burton and the director write Burton's introductory speech. Dinner becomes a last minute discussion with the director about any problems, while the main purpose of a late night supper around 11.30 is to talk about the next day's editing and the links Burton is to record. The next morning at nine o'clock, Tipping, with another director, faces 11 more finalists to repeat the procedure; and so on for the eight days.

'The real problem is not a mechanical one,' says Tipping. 'It's stopping everyone being frayed. By the end of those eight days everybody's on a very short fuse.'

'The recordings have to be done that way because we don't want competitors to be hanging around,' he says. 'We get a chance to catch our breath because there is a three-day gap between those eight days and the Grand Final which is recorded on Saturday for showing on Sunday.'

The series has yielded some pleasant surprises for Tipping. One is that the standard of the music is very high and is getting higher, the other is the popularity of the programme.

'We are showing serious music at peak viewing time, a lot of which is pretty abstruse. There's not too much Tchaikovsky, yet the public seem to like it because it's a competition and, of course, it features young people. We get up to nine million viewers.'

But if the competitors' taste in music is adventurous, their dress sense is very conservative and that is in no way dictated by the BBC.

'If one of them turned up with pink hair, wearing an earring and Hell's Angels clothes, I wouldn't mind at all,' says Tipping.

A television picture from Buckingham Palace of the historic
meeting between The Queen and the Pope on 28 May 1982.

The Papal Visit

Scene from a helicopter of Bella Houston Park, Glasgow.
One of the massive crowds which greeted the Pope.

The Pope arriving at Gatwick.

'The total amount of hardware needed to cover adequately this energetic Pope was beyond the total amount of facilities that either the BBC or ITV possessed,' says Michael Lumley, who was executive producer for the Pope's visit. 'Both we and they would have needed to drop every other television outside broadcast over the six-day period of the visit.'

The Pope's visit prompted an almost ecumenical spirit of unity between the two traditional television rivals and the event was amicably divided between them. This kind of agreement had happened before, to a much lesser degree, in 1966 at the time of the World Cup.

'It made common sense if we and ITV pooled our resources,' continues Lumley. 'So we shook hands to make sensible use of our equipment but retained the right to use the material editorially as we wished.'

'For example, at Westminster Cathedral on the morning of the first Mass celebrated by a Pope in this country, the coverage came from Thames Television,' Lumley explains. 'We did the visit to Canterbury on the second day.'

The BBC covered 10 major sites during the visit and over 100 cameras were used. The entire operation involved approximately 500 people, including engineers and production staff. Independent Television News co-ordinated ITV's coverage using the resources of each ITV company when the Pope was in their area.

'We made available to each other all the pictures but it was left to each organisation to decide whether to transmit them or not or whether to use them as highlights,' says Lumley. 'Each of us used our own commentators so at Westminster Cathedral Tom Fleming was heard over the Thames's pictures and similarly, the commentary of ITN's Alastair Burnet accompanied the BBC's pictures.

'It was a unique set-up for a unique occasion to provide the British public with the best kind of coverage. But we both had our own news coverage independently present.'

'To the Pope or the viewer, the visit was one event,' says Lumley, 'but from the broadcaster's point of view it was a whole series of separate broadcasts, sometimes two or three in a day, that is about 20 individual broadcasts.'

'Some of these were huge in themselves like the visit to Canterbury, some were smaller like his arrival at Gatwick. We also had to cope with the common outside broadcast factor of unpredictability.'

To bring a further dimension of difficulty into this maze of preparations, there was uncertainty until the last moment as to whether the Pope would cancel his visit. This was a result of the Falklands conflict. The Pope did not want the Roman Catholics in Argentina to misinterpret the purpose of his visit to Britain. 'The only assumption we could make was that he would come,' says Lumley. 'It was frustrating not knowing but in practical terms it made no difference.'

Lumley's last major event had been the Royal Wedding.

'The Royal Wedding which was a huge and complicated occasion, had more cameras and was more technically demanding than other events. It was, however, fixed in London,' says Lumley. 'What made the Pope's visit particularly difficult was that it was not geographically confined—it went from Gatwick to Victoria to Buckingham Palace to Westminster Cathedral, for example, with different teams covering every stage of the tour. And many of these took place inside some of the great cathedrals of our nation which needed special lighting.'

The Popemobile in the cargo area of Gatwick Airport.
Below: Open air Mass at Wembley

The Pope and the Archbishop of Canterbury.
Below: The Papal entourage in the precincts of Canterbury Cathedral.

Off-air picture of Hesketh's coverage of the air attack on *Sir Galahad*.

Bernard Hesketh (right) and Jockel at Port Stanley carrying their camera and sound equipment.

Reporter Brian Hanrahan taking a break in the field.

News team (from left to right) Bernard Hesketh, Brian Hanrahan and John Jockel on HMS *Hermes*.

The team interviewing a marine aboard *Hermes*.

**News
in the Falklands**

'I thought it would be a boat trip,' says Bernard Hesketh, the BBC's award-winning news cameraman, who has covered wars in Vietnam, Iran-Iraq, the Middle East and Angola and saw action as a sergeant in the Second World War. 'I didn't think there would be a war. I genuinely thought there would be a negotiated settlement.'

'My feeling about the sense of going to war as against going to show the flag happened when we knew we were being observed by an Argentinian reconnaissance aircraft a couple of days out from Ascension Island.'

It was Palm Sunday and Bernard Hesketh was attending the christening of his six-month-old grandson James Erskine in a village in the heart of the Cambridgeshire countryside. At two o'clock in the afternoon he got a telephone call telling him he had to be down at Portsmouth by midnight to join the Fleet. He and reporter Brian Hanrahan and sound recordist John Jockel would be sailing to the Falklands with the aircraft carrier HMS *Hermes* the following morning, the 5th April.

Within half an hour he was on the road to Television Centre. Like all the best newsmen he always carries an overnight bag and two passports. But he needed to call at the BBC to make a number of changes to the equipment he would take — a lightweight ENG (electronic newsgathering) camera weighing 18lb and a film camera about half that weight. He had to sign an enormous number of papers to do with the Official Secrets Act and get his official documentation as a war correspondent. He took with him 70 rolls of film — about 28,000 feet — and 50 videotapes. He needed both types of camera because the radar on the warships caused massive interference on the ENG video picture.

Bernard Hesketh's first footage of the men on active duty was taken on 1st May. At first light, aircraft took off from *Hermes* to bomb Stanley airstrip, an event immortalised by Brian Hanrahan's now famous phrase: 'I counted them all out and I counted them all back.'

'Brian was standing alongside me on the superstructure above the flight deck of *Hermes*,' says Hesketh, 'and we actually did do that. We were very glad to see the last one return.'

But with the Falklands at least 100 miles away they still seemed distant from the conflict. That was to change on 4th May when the *Sheffield* was hit and finally sank four days later. At only eight to nine miles away, it was easily visible from *Hermes*.

Explains Hesketh: 'I didn't ask for a helicopter trip that first day because I felt it would be unreasonable and might put someone's life at risk. But the next day I did and was refused three or four times even though I knew there were helicopters leaving on observation.'

But the third day he finally got on a helicopter — although neither Hanrahan nor Jockel were allowed on board — with some of the crew and the senior engineering officer of the *Sheffield* who were going aboard to see if it was possible to salvage the ship.

'Just as we were going to take off I was ordered off the helicopter,' he says. 'It was only after a long conversation with Captain Sam Salt of the *Sheffield* that I managed it on the fourth day. He thought it would be a good thing to be able to see the pictures which he could run over and over again to see the extent of the type of damage caused by the Exocet.'

From *Hermes*, the BBC trio changed to the Royal Fleet Auxiliary Supply vessel *Stromness*, packed to the gunwales with ammunition, which was going in with the Assault Fleet to San Carlos water. 'As dawn broke it was quite eerie going in

through Falklands Sound into the narrow neck of the approach to San Carlos water. It was like going down a wide river with mountains on either side,' says Hesketh. 'We could hear some shooting from Fanning Head, where a small detachment of Argentinians was being taken out by our forces. It was a gorgeous morning, bitterly cold with beautiful sunshine and staggering visibility. We were worrying about misjudging distances. Not long after day-break the air raids started and they continued all day. I was on the top deck almost throughout the day. If I had a choice—and you don't as a cameraman—that's where I'd be. I think the bravest men are those below the hatches. They are trapped there. That offensive lasted for a week.'

But it was not until 2nd June—nearly two months after they had sailed out of Portsmouth—that they spent any length of time on land. Then the three went ashore with Five Brigade who were on the southern flank near Goose Green, Darwin and Bluff Cove.

They spent nearly three weeks with Five Brigade. The climax of this period was the major air attack on the landing ship *Sir Galahad* at Fitzroy. This was the biggest single British disaster of the war, and 53 men were lost.

'When it happened I was probably one of the closest people to the ship,' says Hesketh. 'I was just below the hill which overlooks Fitzroy Cove, where the *Sir Galahad* and the *Sir Tristram* were anchored and I was in fact taking pictures of the Fitzroy settlers and the soldiers of the Second Parachute Regiment who were relaxing after their victory at Goose Green before the assault on Stanley. Out of the blue, without any warning, the Mirage and Sky Hawks attacked. The air raid was really very frightening because it was short and sharp. It was all over in a few seconds. What was so horrifying was seeing the casualties being brought in.'

At times like these in wars, mediamen are often fiercely criticised for continuing to do their job.

The vindication of Hesketh's argument is the film he took of the terrible attack at Fitzroy. That such courage and bravery should go unseen would have been a tragedy of a different kind.

But the British public were not allowed to see the final surrender of the Argentinians to the British.

'We were in the mountains,' says Hesketh. 'We got a lift back to Fitzroy and I thought I could get a helicopter into Stanley. But General Moore issued instructions "no Press".'

'This was the result of a decision made in London,' continues Hesketh, a gentle, soft-spoken man of mild manners. 'The view of the MOD at that time was that it might jeopardise the cease-fire arrangements and cause more casualties because Menendez, the Argentinian commander, had been so humiliated.'

'I don't think that view was valid,' he says. 'They were small fry by comparison with the Germans and the Japanese and after all we had filmed both those surrenders. I made my point to Colonel David Dunne, General Moore's public relations officer, that the British people had the right to see this, especially the families of the men who had fought and died, and I was the person who could provide this coverage. It was the only time I really did lose my temper and let rip.'

Bernard Hesketh's coverage of the Falklands War has earned him the 1983 Cameraman of the Year award from the Royal Television Society.

'I'm not a hero or anything like that,' he says. 'Of course I was frightened. If you are not frightened you are a danger to yourself and everyone else.'

A front seat view of Billie Jean King for one of the Centre Court's six BBC cameras, and (*below*) a shot of Chris Evert Lloyd from the same camera.

40

Previous pages: The highest camera position is on the roof of Number One Court. The cameraman must go through the Plant Room and up a ladder to reach it.

A wet Centre Court.

Wimbledon is still considered to be the greatest lawn tennis tournament in the world and as such it commands a huge audience both in Britain and abroad.

Part of its popularity is due to the coverage it gets from the BBC who has exclusive British rights and, as the host broadcaster, supplies most of the material seen abroad.

Each year a miniature Television Centre and temporary 'office block' spring up in the grounds of The All England Club at the end of June for the Wimbledon fortnight.

In the centre of it all sits the master control room, a giant 19-ton van with expanding sides and 30 monitors, in which the co-ordinating producer Martin Hopkins works for up to 12 hours a day.

'If you do my job there is no chance of developing a suntan,' he says, 'quite apart from sitting on the Centre Court and watching any live tennis.' From his van he and the Editor Harold Anderson co-ordinate all the BBC1 and BBC2 coverage.

'As anyone will tell you,' says Hopkins, 'Wimbledon was not built for television. We have had to fit our requirements into the existing structure. Over the years we have increased our output so that now we can have acceptable coverage of courts 2, 3 and 14 as well as the Centre and Number One Courts.'

'Nearly all the BBC's outside broadcast units come off the road for us,' he says. 'We also have six videotape machines, 17 cameras, a tented canteen, our own portable lavatories and miles of cable. It is a vast team effort between production people, engineers and commentators who number close to 200.'

The commentators watch the matches from their box on the court but Harry Carpenter, who introduces and links the

different programmes, spends his Wimbledon underground in a permanent, specially built studio. He hardly sees the light of day and cheerfully refers to himself as 'the mole of Wimbledon'.

Interviews with the players take place some distance away in a small studio alongside the players' dressing-rooms. 'Of all the big sporting events Wimbledon comes nearest to being an on-site affair,' says Martin Hopkins.

'But even with Wimbledon, the evening match of the day has to be edited back at Television Centre,' says Hopkins. 'It is my ambition to see the whole job done at Wimbledon.'

With matches on all 18 courts during the first week, Hopkins has two eagle-eyed spotters with binoculars stationed high on the roofs of Number One Court and the Centre Court. They can see every game and can read the scoreboards. Their observation is backed up by a computer read-out so Hopkins is aware of everything that is going on all the time. The cable circuits to the courts are designed so that cameras can be plugged in to cover the action on any one.

Wimbledon may mean strawberries and cream, but it also means rain.

Hopkins gets regular weather reports. An unofficial, more immediate one comes from the highest man at Wimbledon, the cameraman on the roof of Number One Court. He warns of the approach of dark stormclouds.

'Then our videotape team starts shuffling tapes quicker than a card-school so that we don't run out of material,' says Hopkins. 'It can become very difficult to maintain an acceptable alternative of previously recorded matches when, as happened for a couple of years, rain came down on day one. Then we showed significant matches of other years.'

Cramped conditions for Centre Court commentators John Barrett, (right), Virginia Wade and OB stage manager Bob Clarkson.

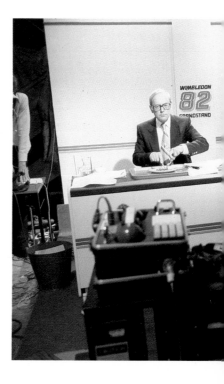

Make-up girl Lesley Smith with Harry Carpenter. *Right:* Lunch in the 'bunker'.

The commentators' view of play on the Centre Court.

David Vine interviews 1982 Ladies' Singles Champion Martina Navratilova.

Behind the polystyrene fort, with the tower made of telegraph poles.

Major de Beaujolais (David Sumner) being made up.

Beau Geste

Beau Geste contains all the classic elements of a *Boy's Own* story—romantic adventure in a foreign land, the triumph of honour and traditional values and a pace which never slackens. But what the author, P. C. Wren, could never have envisaged was that this spirit of derring-do would abound in the BBC Props and Visual Effects Departments which helped make his novel come so vividly to life on the small screen.

'We had genuine Lebel rifles which were used by the French Foreign Legion up to the Second World War,' says director Douglas Camfield, one of the country's leading experts on the Foreign Legion. 'And half the Foreign Legion uniforms were genuine. I think some even had bullet holes. We got them from France and from this country.'

This eight-part BBC1 Classical Serial gave Visual Effects man, Jim Francis, the chance to create spectacular pyrotechnics and explosions. 'I like doing fire sequences because the way we do them is extremely safe and very little can go wrong,' he says. 'You fire-proof everything so that it won't burn but then you have a burning material such as petrol gel which you put where you want the flame to be.'

Francis emphasises that there is never any suggestion that they are playing with fire. 'All our fire sequences are controlled effects and in the case of *Beau Geste* we had the Dorset Fire Brigade on hand as an extra precaution,' he says.

It is essential when dealing with fire that the actor feels safe and at ease. For this reason, Francis demonstrates the use of protective creams which are flame and heat resistant. 'You can put them on your arm and have your arm on fire — not for very long. You are talking about seconds,' he says.

'You do this to show how protective cream works and also show yourself burning,' something of course, which they 45

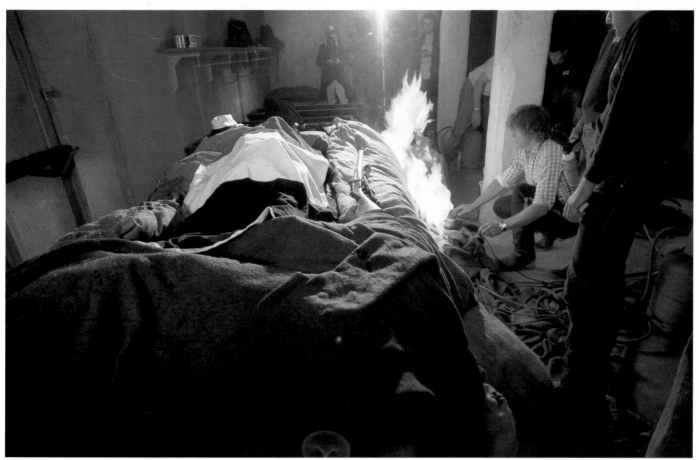

Visual Effects designer Jim Francis adding fuel to the fire from a giant gas burner for the Viking funeral pyre sequence and (*below*) recording the result.

Opposite: Two legionnaires taking a rest in the 'desert', a disused quarry in Dorset.

Petrol gel to enable Digby Geste, actor Anthony
Calf (*below*), to set light instantly to the tower.

Visual Effects man preparing a hole in
the ground for explosive devices.

won't experience. 'They are just going to feel the heat. It's to
get their confidence and show you are not frightened.'

Digby Geste (Anthony Calf) had promised his brother
Beau a Viking's funeral with a spectacular burning pyre. This
provided a double problem for Francis. He had to make sure
that what was meant to take fire sprang instantly into flame—
'the actor didn't want to be standing there forever waiting for
the pillars to burn'—but equally, the whole conflagration had
to be controlled.

A paraffin-soaked torch was placed in a fire-proofed
blanket so Calf knew the flames could not go up his arm.
Where necessary, Francis added bottled gas to the flames.

The most difficult job was setting fire to the fort—Fort
Zinderneuf, a desert outpost in North Africa—represented by
a polystyrene construction, topped by a tower of telegraph
poles, in a disused Dorset quarry.

'Producer Barry Letts wanted as spectacular a bang as
possible,' says Francis. 'But we couldn't blow it up as it was
polystyrene and the fort would just have melted, showing all
the scaffolding bars behind.'

Wooden supports were erected behind the fort and petrol
gel was smeared on top of them so that flames and smoke were
visible without revealing the source of the flame. Explosives
were placed in the middle of the fort in large metal dustbins,
called mortars, which controlled the force and direction of the
explosion. The tower had high explosives around its base but
the whole effect would have been ruined if it had fallen the
wrong way and hit the fort.

'I had three of my men holding a steel cable attached to the
tower to make sure that didn't happen,' says Francis. 'There
are no second takes on a job like this.'

Visual Effects designer Jim Francis preparing the explosive mixture used to blow up the fort, and (*below*) the Dorset Fire Brigade dousing the flames after the event.

Overleaf: Six hours' work by the Visual Effects Team ends in the spectacular burning of Fort Zinderneuf.

Filming the Restoration comedy *The Country Wife* in the seventeenth-century Sheldonian Theatre, Oxford.

Left: Candles and gaslight were supplemented by television lighting for the correct period effect.

All the World's a Stage

Rome was not built in a day but part of it was constructed in 48 hours at Caesar's Camp Rifle Ranges in Farnborough, Hampshire by Jim Clay, a BBC set designer.

This site, some 30 miles from London, was chosen as the best place outside Italy to film a group of actors setting up their stage for a performance of the ancient Roman comedy *The Haunted House* by Plautus.

To a low brick wall on a grassy bank Clay added polystyrene Roman columns and PVC bricks, and he planted a group of 15-foot-tall cypress trees to look like a small corner of the Eternal City. For further effect, he scattered around wicker prop baskets, earthenware jugs and masks, copies of the type which could have been worn by Roman actors of that period.

This 13-part television history of the theatre, which moves from Greek drama to the present day, is presented by playwright Ronald Harwood. It is very much his personal view. Part documentary and part live performance, it focuses on what Harwood calls a series of 'theatrical explosions', periods of intense dramatic activity in various countries at different times.

The comedies of Plautus have a direct link with our bawdier versions today, like *Up Pompeii*, so it was type-casting to put Frankie Howard in *The Haunted House*.

'We showed a small part of an entrance to a Roman villa where a travelling group of players would pitch their stage and perform,' says Clay, 'and then transferred to a modern stage version of *The Haunted House* which was done at the Fortune Theatre in London.'

'The greatest headache of the whole series was making theatre work on television,' he continues. 'My particular problem was making a stage set look just that, but not to the extent that the director is shooting up against the raw edges of

The façade of the Sheldonian Theatre representing the New Theatre, Drury Lane.

the scenery flats,' says Clay. 'Then you would be very aware that it is theatre but it would not be a very interesting picture.'

This kind of dilemma, in another form, faced Keith Cheetham, one of the two directors on the series.

'The first consideration when you are filming a live production is how do you make it remain theatre and not become televised drama,' he says.

'Sometimes you make rules such as never having the camera onstage when there is a proscenium arch,' he says. 'If you do a close-up it must become a close-up in the theatrical sense which sounds like a contradiction because that is a filmic term. The moment a director starts working with a camera he obviously is making a film rather than a piece of theatre. You have to find a compromise somewhere between the two which satisfies the demands of both theatre and television.'

These are demands which actors who regularly perform in

both mediums are now more used to satisfying. But in this series, on occasions, it was necessary for them to return to a declamatory style of delivery, such as that used in the episode on French theatre of the seventeenth century, the age of the great playwrights Corneille, Racine and Molière.

'Molière's *Jeu de Paume* was a tennis court,' says Cheetham, 'a long, narrow building where the actors had to yell their lines to be heard. To be totally authentic, the only thing for our actors to do was to stand downstage centre and shout their heads off. No point in doing a close-up then!'

Another difference between television and the theatre is that vital element, the live audience. In Restoration comedy the audience was an integral part of the performance and consequently, when we came to film the sequence from *The Country Wife*, the audience was cast with as much care as the performers.

53

54

Frankie Howard arriving at the 'Roman villa' in Farnborough, Hampshire, designed by Jim Clay.

Tracking shot of ancient Roman travelling players.
Below: Make-up artist Sylvia Thornton holding the latex rubber masks she made, part of the set dressing.

The first day of the four-day Open Golf Championship, held in 1982 at the Royal Troon Golf Club in Scotland, can be a particularly uncomfortable event for a producer.

There are 150 players hitting off in threes at ten-minute intervals on day one from 7.30 am to 4.15 pm and there is no one obvious person for the television cameras to follow, apart from past champions or those favoured to do well.

The result is that producer Richard Tilling is confined to his large 19-ton mobile control room from early in the morning until eight at night, sustained by coffee and sandwiches, not daring to venture out in case he misses a memorable drive.

'Everything is happening at the same time everywhere, something like 20 matches which need watching at once,' he says. 'When the scores start coming in then you know who to concentrate on, and once the first two days are over, life is much

easier. There are 87 players on the third day and 60 on the fourth.'

'Then you virtually ignore the earlier players because the leaders go last,' he continues. 'The idea is that the last match contains the winner but, of course, it doesn't always happen like that. This was the case in 1982 when Tom Watson of the United States won. He was in the third to last match, but, naturally we had that covered.'

Units came from London, Birmingham and Glasgow in 1982 to cover this event which alternates between Scotland and England. There were 22 cameras and 25 camera positions, as well as a buggy on the course for the cameraman with a lightweight hand-held camera to do personality shots and close-ups. Every hole of the 18 is covered.

'Visually, Troon is like the end of the world,' says Tilling.

Camera overlooking the green at the 8th hole.

Golf: The Open

'You feel as if you could fall off the edge of the world. The winds off the sea make it a very difficult course to play. On many holes you have to have two cameras because they are so long or are shaped like a dog's leg. You have one on the fairway and one on the green, but sometimes it is necessary to have three cameras.'

One of the most dramatic camera positions came from a 70-foot-high hoist behind the grandstand on the 16th green.

The commentators' studio is a specially erected wooden hut, 36 feet long, beside the Clubhouse and it overlooks the 18th hole. It houses Harry Carpenter who does the links with the studio and commentator Peter Alliss, as well as six other commentators. The 18 holes are divided between the commentators.

In 1980 the Royal Troon Golf Club installed a computer to provide detailed information and analysis on the players' performances which is invaluable for the commentators. Every hole is analysed down to the number of birdies, eagles, etc. as well as the average number of strokes played for that hole. As a fail-safe, the complete system is duplicated so there is no chance of a breakdown in the stream of information during the Open.

When two interesting matches are going on at the same time, Tilling follows the person who putts first and stays with that game.

'We don't believe in split screens like the Americans,' he says. 'I do one live and I tell one of the assistant producers to record the other, then when the first is finished I play in the other. Of all the sporting events I cover, not one wrings me dry like the Open does.'

The 36-ft-long wooden hut (*right*) which houses
link man Harry Carpenter and seven commentators.

Buggy which carries cameraman with lightweight unit around the course.

Cameraman on a 70-ft hoist over the 16th hole.

Colourful golfing umbrellas protect the spectators at Troon.

Last of the Summer Wine

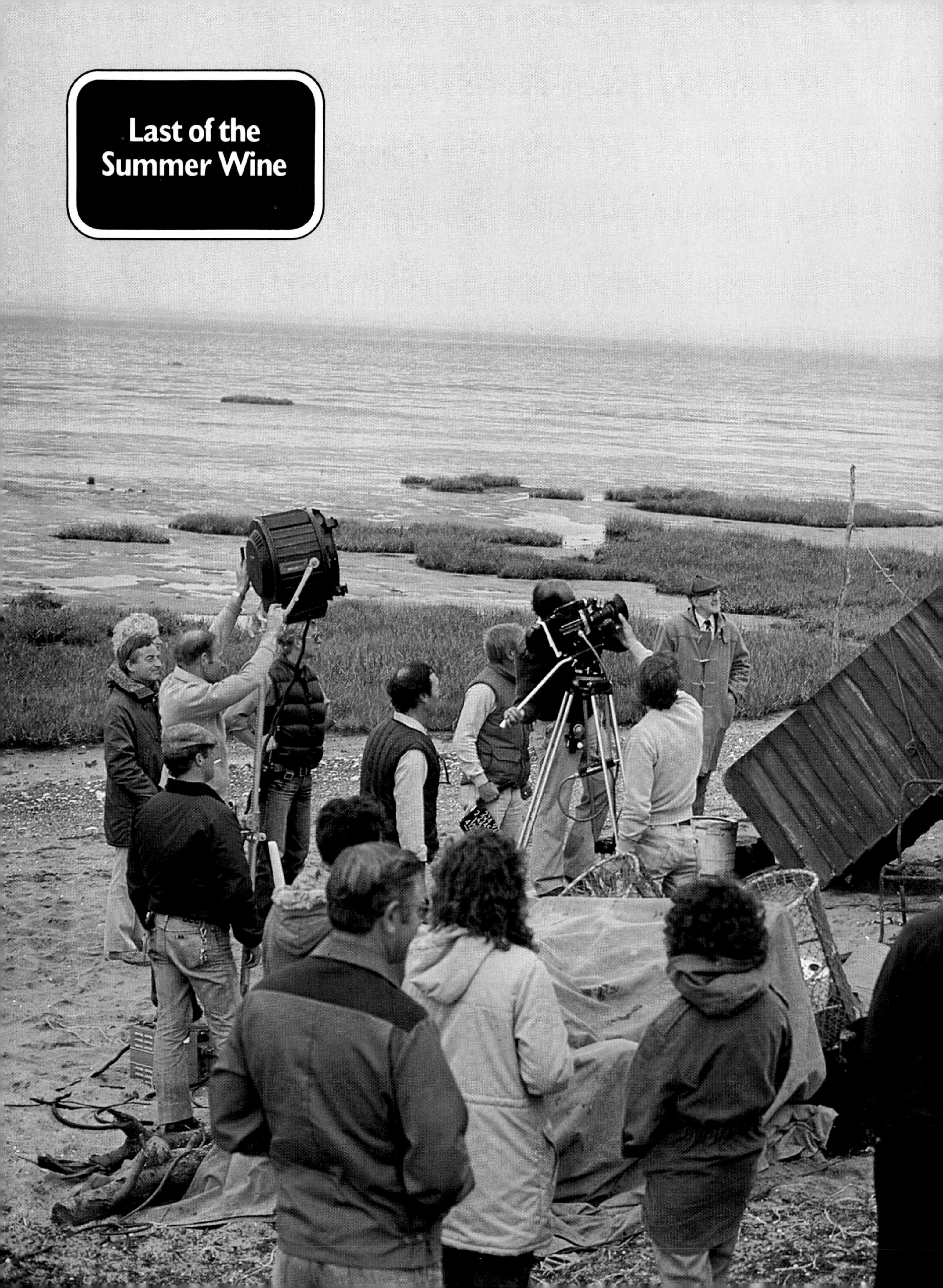

Producer Sydney Lotterby rehearsing Foggy (Brian Wilde), Compo (Bill Owen) and Clegg (Peter Sallis).
Below: The large plastic sheet normally used to reflect light is used as a wind and rain shield.

Previous pages: Recording a stunt sequence involving Compo (Bill Owen) at Spurn Head promontory, Hull.

Cameraman Max Sammett filming while Sydney Lotterby watches the result on his video view-finder.

Three old codgers, one lusting after a middle-aged woman in rollers and baggy stockings, would seem unlikely stars to beat *Gone with the Wind*'s Vivien Leigh and Clark Gable in the ratings. But since Christmas 1981, Clegg (Peter Sallis), Foggy (Brian. Wilde) and Compo (Bill Owen) have consistently proved their popularity by staying at the top of the 20 favourite programmes on British television, with an audience of around 16 million.

It was not always like this. Ever since the pilot episode in 1972, the show had attracted a devoted but small audience of about three million. The BBC is as keen as any commercial company for its share of the ratings but this is not the only criterion used when deciding whether a show is a success and if it should be taken off the air. The BBC not only has an enviable record for initiating highly original comedy but also for having the courage to allow 'a slow burner', as producer/director Sydney Lotterby calls it, time to establish itself.

Certainly, the people of Holmfirth, the village where much of the series is filmed, were not early fans. Writer Roy Clarke discovered that they used to turn down the sound and just watch their beautiful Yorkshire scenery. All that has changed now, and they are among the keenest viewers. The countryside may look lovely from the warmth and comfort of one's favourite armchair but more often than not it provides a chilly, wet location for the production team.

In conditions like this, Lotterby, always working to a tight schedule, finds himself doing what no scientist has yet managed to do—changing the weather to suit his current need. 'We take our own sun with us,' says Lotterby, 'in the form of an arc light.' A 12-foot-square piece of plastic attached to a frame is hoisted into place as a windshield or a roof. So while on either side the drizzle comes down, underneath it looks like a fine day on film. In fact, when the sun does shine, that does not suit either. 'We have to soften the sun,' says Lotterby. 'Sunlight is so hard it causes tremendous contrasts so we put fine gauze over the frame which still gives the contrasts but not so harshly.'

One of the delights of the series is seeing our three characters as tiny figures in the landscape, ruminating on life, the state of Compo's wellies or Mrs Batty's intransigence. Each one speaks his lines into a radio mike with Lotterby perhaps a quarter of a mile away. 'But that causes problems,' he says, 'because it means coping with three times as much extraneous noise.'

Once again, Sydney Lotterby finds taming the elements—in this case the wind—one of his prime tasks. Microphones used outside can have up to three layers of gags around them. The first is a rigid nylon mesh cage which cuts down the sound of the microphone itself going through the air; a sponge rubber gag is added to combat high winds; and finally if a gale is looming both of these are encased in a woolly sock of cotton and furry man-made fibres.

The weather has another effect on the production. 'We get two distinct performances from the actors,' says Lotterby. 'There is a difference between saying the lines to themselves in the cold in Yorkshire when perhaps it is raining and saying them in the warmth of a television studio with the additional warmth of the audience reaction. It would be so much more helpful if we could take the audience to Yorkshire. On the other hand, it would be better if we could put it all on film, after all, it is a comedy set mainly out of doors.'

Sydney Lotterby with Compo (centre) and his double
Stuart Fell, stuntman on six of the seven series to date.

The mattress inside the caravanette to break Fell's fall.

'Compo' about to fall.

64

Summertime Special combines two essential elements for a show business success—the romance of life under the big top with all its traditional associations, and the glamour of the big stars.

In 1982 the BBC pitched its huge tent at Eastbourne and took up residence on the front in Princes Park for the summer season. Eastbourne is near enough to London to allow such stars as Shirley Bassey, Bernie Winters, Lulu, Janet Brown, Buck's Fizz, Vince Hill and Max Bygraves to travel down from the capital.

It is more economical to remain in one place rather than break up camp every couple of weeks to move to other seaside resorts. Another advantage is that it makes it worthwhile to spend time enlarging the stage and technical areas, which gives the producer, Stewart Morris, conditions of near studio quality, although limited space reduces the audience from 1400 to 800.

It also means that the production team only have to suffer the agony of the tent being put up once, although with a force five gale blowing non-stop at Eastbourne for a day that was anxiety enough.

'It's a 24-hour operation watching the tent, continually loosening and tightening the ropes depending on what the weather is like,' says Geoff Jowitt, senior production manager.

If Morris is the man who makes things happen inside the tent, Jowitt is the person who sees that the show can go on at all. A recent change in a by-law meant that for the first time a singing and dancing licence—at the princely sum of 25p—had to be applied for. In an open court before a magistrate, representatives from the police, the fire brigade and the local council had to decide whether there were any objections to the BBC being granted such a licence. 'In the past if you weren't charging money you didn't need to have a licence,' says Jowitt. 'Luckily one of the local people I was dealing with pointed out it was now necessary to apply for one, and that's how I came to go to court for the BBC.'

Summertime Special regularly featured a group of dancers known as the 'A' team whose routines were vivid and fast moving. To capture this to greatest effect, a Nike camera crane which can move at up to 30 mph was used.

'It's a 'very' versatile camera crane,' says Jowitt, which gives excellent manoeuvrability and adjustment of shots, swinging easily from lateral to vertical. It can move back very quickly from a close-up and you can get lovely developing shots: it's ideal for dancers. We hired ours as they are in very short supply: there are only about three in the country.'

'Although using it was a great success, it did have one drawback: the crane's track lost us 300 seats. Television in a tent does have its ups and downs.'

Television in a tent. Make-up cabin (left) and (right) caravans used for artists' dressing-rooms.

Summertime
Special

Bernie Winters and his St Bernard, Snorbitz.

No. 1 camera position, a mole crane.

Shackleton

Mark Williams, assistant floor manager, packing up his props as an ice storm approaches.

For eight months of the year, Angmagssalik on the east coast of Greenland is totally cut off from the world—it does not even have television! In March and July last year it was filled with a BBC film crew of around 30 people. They took all 12 beds in the only hotel, fondly dubbed the Portakabin for its dissimilarity to the Savoy, while the rest were billeted in empty council houses.

Nowadays no one is surprised that people should want to go to the end of the world—in this case both ends—to re-create one of man's most incredible feats of endurance.

For if Shackleton, played in this four-part series by David Schofield, was a failure as an explorer, his achievement in human terms was unparalleled, particularly in his four attempts to rescue his 22 men stranded on Elephant Island 800 miles from South Georgia in the Falklands.

Even so, for producer John Harris, writer Christopher Ralling and director Martyn Friend, who had all worked on another outstanding drama-documentary *The Voyage of Charles Darwin*, the making of *Shackleton* ranks as an exceptional achievement. It became a two-year £1½ million odyssey.

'We couldn't go south because it would have been too costly,' says Harris, 'and the back-up required was impossible.'

'We decided to do the ice work and the ship work in the Northern Hemisphere, but we felt the terrain of South Georgia was so distinct with its mountains, glaciers and the

The crew on an ice floe off the east coast of Greenland.

Actor David Schofield as Shackleton.

whaling station that we needed to do some filming there.'

An arrangement was made with the Royal Navy's ice patrol vessel, HMS *Endurance* (named after Shackleton's ship), and a minimal crew—even Harris was excluded—was allowed on board for what was thought to be her last voyage. The Falklands conflict a few months later changed all that, but by that time filming was completed. Equity, the actors' union, gave a special dispensation to allow the ship's crew to double for the actors, none of whom went to the South Atlantic. These long shots were later cut in with close-ups of the actors in Greenland.

Before the unit set out to work in these Arctic conditions they were thoroughly briefed about coping with the environment by the British Antarctic Survey team. This prevented casualties but there were professional problems to be solved. The make-up girls found that the spirit gum froze in seconds when they were sticking on beards so they had to get extra close to the actors. 'It looked as if a number of affairs were developing,' says Harris.

The other cosmetic problem was continuity. It might be months between an actor being filmed outside his tent in the snow and inside it in the studio. Instead of real snow a mixture of icing sugar and desiccated coconut was painted on beards and clothes, and cornflakes made faces look frost-bitten.

The Baltic trading vessel *Søren Larsen*, which was seen as James Onedin's flagship in *The Onedin Line*, took the part of *Endurance*. Moored in Brightlingsea, Essex, she had her hull 69

Lightweight, quarter-scale polystyrene model of *Endurance* built by Visual Effects Department, North Acton.

sheathed in metal before sailing to Greenland. But history came dangerously close to repeating itself before she reached Angmagssalik a week late. Shackleton's *Endurance* had been stuck fast in the ice of the Weddell Sea for ten months and had eventually sunk, crushed by the huge moving ice slabs. The *Søren Larsen* found herself almost trapped between tons of ice floes; she could travel less than one mile in an hour.

On the first day of filming—at a ski resort in the Cairngorms—the crew awoke to find all the snow on their chosen location had been blown away. 'You could see tufts of heather,' says Harris. Determined not to waste the day's filming a new location was found in a car park at the foot of the ski lift. A couple of borrowed sheets from a local hotel gave the impression of snow and the unit was able to film Shackleton arriving at Scott's tent in the Antarctic!

Storms and the South Atlantic are virtually synonymous and they are notoriously difficult to film. One of the storms in *Shackleton* 'took place' on a film stage at Ealing with the model of the boat being drenched on a rocking scaffolding frame. Another occurred at the end of Penarth Pier in Wales.

'It's always difficult to get boat shots which are believable and controlled,' says Harris. 'The principle in going to the end of a pier is that you can have a pontoon or another boat moored to it and film from that. It had to be very rough so we had huge wind machines like aeroplane propellers blowing a gale with hose pipes and a speed boat zipping up and down to churn up the water.'

An old lady watching in fascination wanted to know why they chose Penarth Pier. 'Was it because it was like the piers in the South Atlantic?' she asked.

Another model, the Chilean tug *Yelcho*, positioned by nylon lines from a rowing boat.

Opposite: The *Endurance*, played by the Danish vessel *Søren Larsen*, making its way through the pack ice.

Plastic tent over the camera while setting up a shot of a waterfall.

Director Martyn Friend (top) setting up a high-angled shot from *Endurance*, with grips Malcolm Sheehan (right) and cameraman David Whitson.

Helicopter ferried 15 people and eight dogs to glacier for ice-shelf sequences.

The British Antarctic Survey team advised the crew to wear dark glasses, especially in dull weather.

Creating a setting Antarctic sun in Greenland for a shot in which Australian cameraman Frank Hurley, on the Shackleton expedition, takes his famous photograph.

One of the principal cameras used for a wide-angle shot of the Royal Albert Hall, and (*below*) the BBC Symphony Orchestra rehearsing.

'It's not really a music programme, it is a carnival,' says Rodney Greenberg, producer of *The Last Night of the Proms*. 'For me the audience are the stars of the programme. People like "Loony Ken" who conducts with a baton he says belonged to Sargent. He has been to a thousand Proms and wears himself out. We always show him. He is a fixture. He is there for every concert. But where does he go for the rest of the year? I believe he works in a furniture factory in Twickenham.'

Greenberg's favourite camera position is high up beside the organ pipes because it gives a fine view of the Prommers' faces. 'A full frontal of the screaming hordes and all their banners waving,' is how he puts it. It also shows the relationship between the conductor and the Prommers. They are separated by a small space known as No Man's Land which, due to the Prommers' great enthusiasm, is only just prevented from being invaded. The one person allowed in there is a cameraman who inevitably appears on our screens at some time during the evening so he must wear a black tie to be appropriately dressed for the occasion.

The Prommers may be the stars of the show but they can cause headaches for the producer and especially for the presenter, who is particularly vulnerable out there in the front line. After all, the producer is outside the building watching it all in his mobile control room. 'We have never attempted to isolate the presenter by putting a glass screen around the box in which he is perched, facing a camera,' says Greenberg. 'But the Prommers are ruthless in the way they react and ad lib.'

He tells the horrifying story of what they did to Cormack Rigby, Head of Radio 3 Presentation when he was presenting a live Prom simultaneously on Radio 3 and BBC2. They managed to get a copy of his script earlier in the day and made 50 photocopies at South Kensington tube station. As he began his broadcast that evening, the Prommers started reading out their copies as well.

'It became louder and louder and then gradually out of sync with Cormack,' Greenberg recalls. 'They were down there yelling and you just had to stay on the air. The noise was overpowering, but Cormack just smiled and refused to be thrown. On such occasions we have had to try and fade down the Prommers and bring the presenter's voice up to compensate, but there isn't much else you can do.'

Television is still very much Radio's younger sister when it comes to broadcasting concerts. BBC Radio has run the Promenade Concerts since 1927. This has not only guaranteed their continued existence but has built up a tradition which has become inextricably woven into the cultural fabric of our nation. 'Television has to go to Radio to get clearance for some of our requirements,' says Greenberg. 'The quality of the transmission for the listener is always the most important consideration. I don't want to make it sound as though we are being persecuted by an anti-TV bias, but you can't pretend that moving television cameras and lights into a concert doesn't

change things for the people in the hall. We try to keep any nuisance to a minimum. I like to think of it as high-intensity eavesdropping.'

Up to six cameras are used and their positions are strictly regulated by the Albert Hall. Cameras are never moved during a performance. 'I've seen that done at concerts in Israel and America,' says Greenberg. 'For the audience in the hall it becomes almost like watching a hockey match.'

Rodney Greenberg believes any disturbance suffered by the audience of some 7000 souls is counterbalanced by the vast numbers—as many as eight million on the last night—who watch the Proms on the small screen. He also enjoys the

Presenter Richard Baker festooned by Prommers' streamers.

Dinner-jacketed cameraman in 'No Man's Land'.

Conductor James Loughran acknowledges the audience while Prommer 'Loony Ken' continues to 'conduct'.

opportunity of showing the building to those in the auditorium as well as those at home. 'Under normal circumstances there's not enough light to see it properly,' he explains. 'I try and express something about the confident Victorian grandeur of the architecture by arranging lights to highlight such details as organ pipes or gallery arches.'

This means the temperature inside the Albert Hall soars, especially if it coincides with a hot summer night. This was the situation in 1974 which led to the case of the Famous Fainting Baritone.

In the midst of André Previn conducting *Carmina Burana*, Thomas Allen buckled at the knees and passed out from the heat. Fortunately for him—but unfortunately for the musicians—his understudy Christopher Hood was a doctor and felt that it was his duty to accompany Allen to hospital rather than to replace him on stage. History does not relate whether a cry went out, 'Is there an understudy in the house?'

Nevertheless, Patrick McCarthy, a former student of the London Opera Centre, stepped out of the audience, into a borrowed dinner jacket and on to the stage. To Previn's bewilderment and relief, he sang through to the end of the performance, and was given a tremendous ovation. We can only be grateful that television was there to record one man's remarkable musical achievement.

**The Old Men
at the Zoo**

The outside broadcast unit in the grounds of the wildlife park at Cricket St Thomas.

'I think good novels make better television,' says Jonathan Powell, producer of the BBC2 Classic Serial and responsible for two of television's best works over the last few years *Tinker, Tailor, Soldier, Spy* and its sequel *Smiley's People.*

With Betty Willingale, his script editor, Powell has an unrivalled reputation for transferring classics such as *The Mayor of Casterbridge, Crime and Punishment* and *The Barchester Chronicles* to the small screen. But he is equally dedicated to producing contemporary classics for television like Le Carré's two books, Iris Murdoch's *The Bell* and *Testament of Youth* by Vera Brittain.

'I am concerned to broaden out the idea of the classic serial to contemporary fiction and into the contemporary world while retaining the traditional values,' he says. 'This is to make a pact with the original to preserve the uniqueness of the book which is what gives the resultant television fiction its strength.'

'The first thing to go in television is originality,' he continues. 'The moment you start making television there are constraints. I see fiction as a bulwark against the economic demands of television.'

The delicate matter of adapting a novel for television, particularly one which enjoys the tag 'classic', is often seen to the purists as a provocative act. With *The Old Men at the Zoo*, Angus Wilson's fable set a few years in the future—the television version will coincide with the author's seventieth birthday this year—Powell says: 'The scripts have the same characters and the same story but it it not a slavish recreation of the novel Wilson wrote in the Sixties.'

'A lot of the political background we have had to change,' says Powell, 'and the last episode is largely the invention of Troy Kennedy Martin, the script writer. But it is all in accord with Angus Wilson's version. We haven't got away from the spirit of his intention.'

'We are trying to create something which preserves the individuality and the special worth of that book. I think you have a moral duty to consult the novelist. Often you find the novelist is open to change.'

Angus Wilson, who lectured Powell on Virginia Woolf at the University of East Anglia, did not want to do the television adaptation. But he saw the drafts and was kept in touch all the way through. 'There is a special skill in the dramatic organisation of the book into something which works in terms of television,' says Powell. 'Organising the novel material successfully whilst retaining the essence that you want, comes from being a television dramatist and knowing what works, which possibly a novelist does not.'

Like three of Powell's productions, *The Old Men at the Zoo* was all done on location video which is much cheaper than film. The lower cost was one of the main reasons for the choice, but Powell explains why it was especially beneficial for this production, much of which was shot on location at London Zoo. 'Video has a freshness and energy and a largeness of life both in imagery and performances,' says Powell. 'Tape gives a harder edged image; you don't get the perfect modulation or sensitivity you get on film.'

The most difficult part of the entire production was dealing with the animals at Cricket St Thomas in Somerset, the second location. Powell and his crew were totally in the hands of Chipperfield's Circus from whom they hired the lions, panthers, zebras and leopards. There was even a lion-tamer on hand with two pistols. The young men at the circus were taking no chances.

80

Previous pages: Andrew Cruickshank (Sanderson, Curator of Insects) being beaten up.

Tracking shot along a corridor in the Reptile House at London Zoo. Actors (left to right) James Grant, Stuart Wilson and Marius Goring. *Below:* Caged cameraman facing rhinoceros.

Building an amphitheatre in post-nuclear Britain.
Below: Caged girl punks, plus (left) a lion-
tamer for their safety. He turned actor for the
day and was made up to look like one of them.

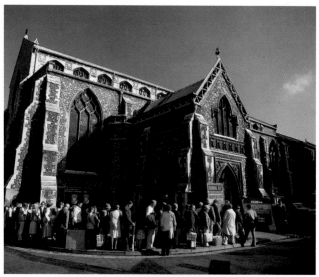

3000 people queued for admission to the show.

Antiques Road Show

Hugh Scully introducing the programme.

Since the *Antiques Roadshow* first set out from Bristol in 1977, well over a quarter of a million people have had the privilege of consulting an expert about a treasured possession.

True, not all have had the good luck to make a fortune, unlike the American couple who bought a box of china in Saigon which included a small blue-grey jug, thrown in as a make-weight. It turned out to be a Ming monk's cap wine ewer which sold for £13,500.

In every town where the 'Roadshow' stops to record a programme, there is always a long queue of people, carrier bags in hand, waiting well before the doors open at 10 am. By 3.30 when the doors close, Arthur Negus and the 20 experts between them will have seen on average 3000 members of the public. The highest turnout was over 7000 in St Austell, Cornwall.

But the purpose of the *Antiques Roadshow* is not just to find the gem amid domestic paraphernalia.

'There is a graded scale and a mix of different things,' says the producer Robin Drake, the man who suggested the idea for the programme. 'I like a third of the items to be the kind that anybody watching could feel they could have had contact with. Others are there from a pure degree of excellence, and also because it's very difficult for an expert to speak at length about something fairly ordinary. And thirdly, I look for entertaining things.'

In one day, between 28 and 32 pieces are recorded, of which 20 may be used. As soon as the public come into the hall they go to Reception and are handed a ticket and told which expert to see.

'You need a good intelligence network,' says Drake. 'The people on the reception desk are informed about antiques without being high-level experts and they let me know when something interesting comes in.'

'The experts will pick out the good items anyway,' he says. 'They all have radio mikes and I eavesdrop on conversations in case there is a quirky or unusual piece which they may not think suitable.'

'Often it's just a gut reaction,' he says. 'Certain people look like good subjects. I have to find the odd, interesting or unusual for the balance of the programme.'

There is no rehearsing the *Antiques Roadshow*, therefore Robin Drake must be aware of everything that is going on around him as it happens on the day. He must also remember the emphasis of earlier programmes so that there is not too much repetition of particular kinds of objects.

For this reason he stays as close to the activity on the floor as possible. At Norwich, there was a curtained-off gallery above the main hall which meant he could watch the two television monitors in a quiet, undistracting environment.

'I need to be close because I may have to dart on to the floor to make a point to an expert or have something re-recorded,' says Drake.

When any item is recorded three cameras are used, one for the expert, one for the owner and a third for the item itself.

People who come for advice are under no obligation to appear in the programme, and Drake always asks if they are willing to be recorded.

Undoubtedly, one of the major reasons the *Antiques Roadshow* has been such a great success is Arthur Negus. In 1983, aged 80, he announced his retirement from the programme.

'We're not replacing him because that would be impossible,' says Drake. 'We'll be like a football team, just playing with the ten remaining men.'

Arthur Negus admiring a woman's William IV wooden wool-winder.
Below: Producer Robin Drake is close at hand for any on-the-spot editorial decisions.

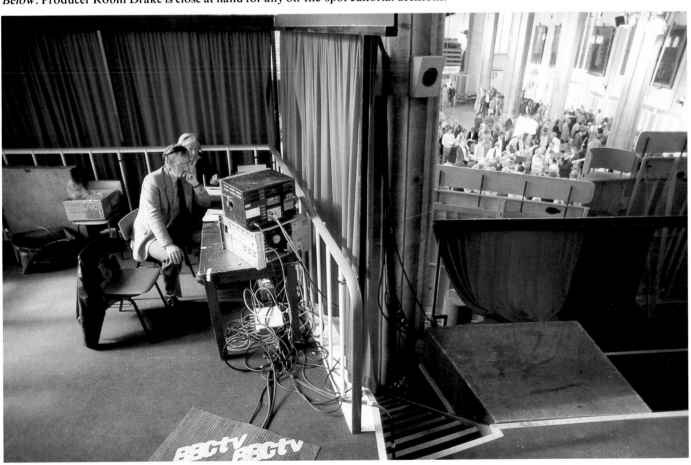

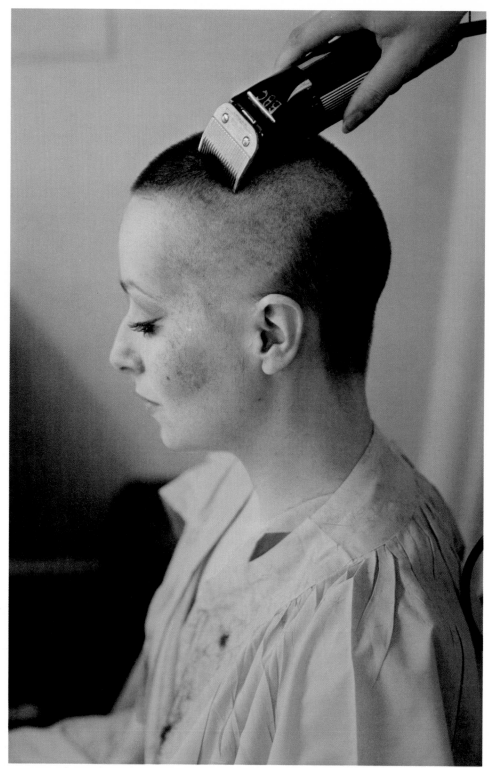

Amanda Boxer (Cleopatra Tryphaena I) having her head shaved for her death scene.

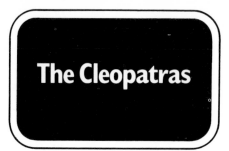

The Cleopatras

Make-up artist Norma Hill and her assistants made all the wigs worn in the production.

The Cleopatras did not set out to be a realistic piece of costume drama 'but a witty, theatrical examination of power', says producer Guy Slater.

Writer Philip Mackie, that skilled creator of such television classics as *The Naked Civil Servant*, wrote it in the style of a horror comic and gave his characters crisp, colloquial dialogue. 'How are you this morning?' asked Potbelly (Richard Griffiths) of his latest conquest Cleopatra III (Michelle Newell), his stepdaughter and soon to become his wife. 'Pregnant,' she replied.

The actors were called upon to give larger than life performances, in keeping with the spirit of outrageousness which Slater, Mackie and director John Frankau were determined to capture. The inclusion of bare-breasted ladies of the court was not part of this spirit of outrageousness 'That was the way they dressed,' says Slater. 'There was nothing erotic about it.'

'*The Cleopatras* didn't take itself seriously. It was a hard-hitting, unsentimental look at a tribe of fairly repellent people. We took dramatic licence to give the necessary verve and gusto. We didn't want the series to have a quiet domestic naturalism to it,' he continues. 'No dead hand of realism with palm trees or shots of the Nile. Historically accurate but not reverential.'

It was all shot in the studio. The set designed by Michael Young consisted of exotically painted interlocking pillars 20 feet high, flights of stairs and a variety of curtains to divide the space into rooms.

In charge of the 18 make-up girls for this production was the make-up designer, Norma Hill. Their job also involved making the wigs and beards. Norma spent two months in the

Reading Room of the British Museum researching the beauty secrets of the Ancient Egyptians.

'I learnt to my horror that they used to take off all their body hair and all the men and some of the women shaved their heads,' she says. 'It is not absolutely known why, but it is believed to be partly for convenience because it was a hot country, but it could have been for ritual. I had to discuss with the director whether it would be better to have bladders [false bald patches] or shaven heads. We decided it would not be practical for crownings and bed scenes so all the artists had to be shaven to the top of the ears. He made the very brave decision where necessary to shave their heads—children as well.'

The only actress to have all her hair shaved off was Amanda Boxer who played Cleopatra Tryphaena I. Her decision to lose her shoulder-length tresses, however, was dramatic rather than cosmetic. In a particularly humiliating death scene she said a shaven head would make her feel even more abject and degraded. The 15 actors who had their heads shaved had look-alike wigs made so that loss of hair would not mean loss of work.

With 50 actors to make up each day, a 6.30 am call was necessary. Apart from facial make-up, some required full body paint, gilded nipples or stencils applied around the neck. In addition, Chickpea (David Horovitch) needed four hours to have the foam latex prosthetic pieces applied to turn him into a baggy-eyed, scraggy-necked 65-year-old. 'The material is like tissue paper and you have to use tweezers to lift and stick the edges otherwise they roll back and create a hard edge which the camera would pick up,' says Norma. 'We joke that we're not brain surgeons but we need almost as steady a hand.' 87

Make-up artist Norma Hill (right) applying decorative collar stencil to one of the Nubian slave extras and (*below*) putting the finishing touches to another of the 30 slaves.

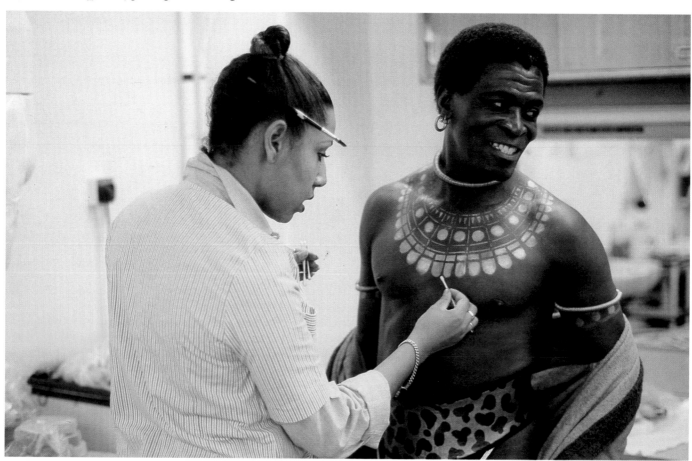

Patrick Troughton (Sextus) checking his Roman wig.
Below: David Horovitch (Chickpea) being 'aged'.

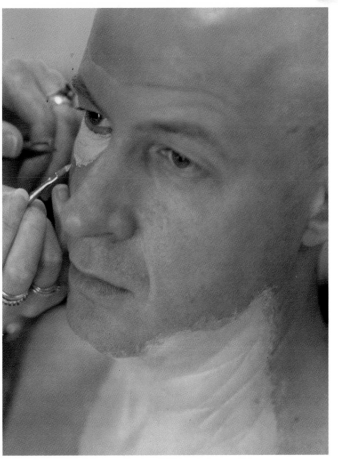

wn locally as the Queen of Beaujolais.

t usually come corked
led 'Fleurie'. For the
he programme resear-
nded by bottles of
oblem but a problem

2-part series about the
ormidable 83-year-old
Cave Coopérative of
president of a wine
cally as the Queen of
ve from her father, its

'but we didn't want a
urie area bring their
ed and tested for sugar
sent down the road to

ert is a great believer
ast a bottle of it daily.
the same thing. 'You
ed an insult. I put on
film. It could be very
'e soon realised that it
rview with her in the

Chabert nine months
lt she would make an

wanted someone who
ho would just do the

producer's bidding or alternatively put on a special performance for the camera.'

'The seeds of success or failure lie in the initial choice
because the whole story comes out of that person,' Laura
continues. 'My only interest is to put characters on the screen
who come across as if you know them.My first questions are
about love and marriage,' she says. 'When I first met Mlle
Chabert she told me how many proposals she had had and
why she had declined them. The way she related them was very
amusing and I said that was the sort of thing we would talk
about in the interview but she said "never" and she was saying
that right up until the interview.'

When it came to the recording, however, she did speak
about this part of her life much to everyone's delight.

'This emphasises the importance of building up a relationship with the person you are interviewing,' says Laura. 'We
spent a lot of time with her socially and she trusted us. I never
use a tape recorder when I am interviewing because I think
people respond better without one. I don't go trying to
squeeze out information but go as a friend and hope the
conversation will flow easily as a result.'

Often the result on screen is so natural that not only the
interviewee but the viewer also forgets the presence of a film
crew. In documentary making it is obviously better to keep the
number to a minimum and Jonathan used a cameraman, a
camera assistant and a sound recordist but no lights. 'This was
partly because lights are very obtrusive,' he says. 'If you are
trying not to be noticed you can be more discreet without
them. And without lights the end result looks very natural. We
used the new fast film stock which shoots at very low light
levels and there was virtually nowhere we couldn't film.'

Cameraman Ian Stone filming an informal wine tasting.
Below: Producer Jonathan Gili (right) with his film crew in the local market.

The weekly family Sunday lunch (*above and below*) with sound recordist Simon Wilson (above right).
Below right: Researcher Laura Gavshon discusses the day's schedule with Mademoiselle Chabert.

A wine tasting where the best years of Fleurie are sampled.
Below: Mademoiselle Chabert sitting in her kitchen.

THE RESOLUTE APPROACH

Commentators' desk at the 1982 Brighton conference.

Conservative Party Conference

'No member of Her Majesty's Government has ever done this to me before,' spluttered an angry Sir Robin Day. He was left with an empty studio after the furious exit of John Nott, then Defence Secretary, but now a knight like Day, who threw down his microphone and stormed out when Sir Robin called him a 'here today and gone tomorrow' politician.

That event was shown on all news bulletins, as well as *Nationwide* and *Newsnight* and is the kind of thing which gives a special zest to Editor Margaret Douglas's job. She is responsible for all BBC live coverage of the four political party conferences as well as those of the TUC and CBI. 'A great slog of time,' she calls it.

'One of the reasons I enjoy covering them so much is that somehow the emotional temperature out of London is higher and everything is a bit more spontaneous and relaxed than when the politicians are back at Westminster,' she says.

Although she puts in a 19-hour day, rising at 7 am to read the papers and not returning to her room until the early hours of the following morning having seen *Newsnight* to bed first, she thinks it is essential that one person should do all the conferences. 'You really do have to pace yourself very carefully,' she says. 'You couldn't do it if you said "this is such hard work" and expected a different team to do each one. The points to compare and contrast would be lost totally.'

'With the Tories in power, theirs is more of a rally than a decision-making process,' says Miss Douglas. 'Their conference is comparatively straightforward in that they stick to their agenda and they run to time so it's a fairly easy problem.'

'Editorially, the Labour Party is more difficult,' she says. 'It is extremely complicated procedurally and keeping in step with what it is doing is usually our main problem.'

The difference between this and most other outside broadcasts is that the Editor, and producer, in this case Colin Martin, stay in the hall where the event is happening rather than in the OB van outside. They work from the commentators' desk, directly opposite the politicians' platform, which, apart from being occupied by Sir Robin Day and David Dimbleby, also seats the researcher Linda Anderson. Her role is to feed the commentators with precise information, plus supplying background material about the speakers or the issue under discussion.

'We feel you need to be in the hall to get the atmosphere and the full flavour of what is happening,' says Miss Douglas. 'This would be hard to detect by only seeing the politicians through your cameras. I am in contact with the OB director outside and I can lead him on the kind of pictures we need to tell the story. Most of the time one doesn't have to, but we always have the ability to do it if we detect some undercurrent which should be revealed.'

The other advantage of being on the spot is that when a story is developing on the floor of the hall the producer or researcher can go down immediately and speak to the relevant people and brief the commentators accordingly.

Margaret Douglas is able to view all the pictures on the desk in front of her. This includes the output of the two cameras in the studio where the interviews are done and the four cameras in the hall, as well as anything recorded on videotape, while another monitor shows ITV. 'I can see anything that is happening anywhere just by pressing a button,' she says.

BBC TV covers most of the conference live. The only programme allowed to interfere with the transmission is *Playschool* from 11 to 11.25 each morning. The cameras are still at work during this time so that edited highlights can be transmitted later.

Commentators Sir Robin Day and David Dimbleby listening to the proceedings.
Below: Margaret and Dennis Thatcher followed by the media on a walkabout.

Part of the production team at work during the conference.
Below: Editor Margaret Douglas briefing her team.

Live coverage is a spin-off from news coverage. 'It developed because these are important occasions which you want to cover for news and in order to do that you need a sizeable operation,' says Miss Douglas. 'So it was decided to make full use of that and broadcast live. This started happening in the early Sixties when we moved from film to VT.'

Margaret Douglas is not only editorially responsible for broadcasting the conferences. This live coverage also provides the raw material for news bulletins and current affairs programmes, so she must make sure that when shown in extract it is true in style and content to its unabridged form.

Autumn is conference time. It starts at the beginning of September with the TUC and ends early in November with the CBI but planning and acquiring the vast amount of space needed begin in January.

'For the Tories in Brighton we still had to spend some thousands of pounds on construction of a set of offices for radio and television plus a television studio even though the building was built as a conference centre,' she says. 'In Blackpool we build all this in what for the rest of the year is a garage.'

As it turned out, this was the last gathering of the Tory faithful before the 1983 General Election, when Thursday, 9th June turned out to be the biggest night of the year for News and Current Affairs. Their coverage started at 10.40 pm on BBC1 led by David Dimbleby and Sir Robin Day with Peter Snow in charge of the computer graphics. In all, 2000 BBC staff were involved, which included 500 reporters stationed at constituency counts around the country. *Election 83* finished at 4 am and coverage resumed with the 6 am start of *Breakfast Time* with Nick Ross, Frank Bough and Selina Scott.

Sir Robin Day interviewing John Nott, then Defence Secretary, minutes before his angry exit. The BBC studio is in constant use for regional and network programmes. *Above:* **The BBC production office.**

Captain Zep (Paul Greenwood) in the blue
the camera does not see.

Zep with Professor Spiro (Harriet Keevil) and
Ben Ellison (Jason Brown) in composite picture.

Captain Zep: Space Detective

'Captain Zep is an honorary role which you mature into,' says
its producer, Christopher Pilkington. 'It's a bit like being
Prime Minister.'

In the first series, Paul Greenwood played Zep, the world's
greatest space detective. He is the creation of Dick Hills, who
used to write for Morecambe and Wise and appeared on their
earlier shows as one of the two stooges. He wrote Zep as a

tongue-in-cheek space adventure.

Pilkington was determined that the series would not remind
viewers either of *Dr Who* or *Blake's Seven.*

'We wanted to expand the imagination and create the
impression that you are watching a comic-strip hero but one
who comes to life as a real super-hero,' says Pilkington. 'But
rather than make the whole thing a comic strip, we decided to
mix the conventions and have Captain Zep and his two
assistants as real live characters.'

'They live and travel around in a real set which is their
space-craft and when they leave that they go into a totally
drawn and stylised environment. That's when they have
entered the world of drama and have gone into an alien
planet.'

BBC graphic designer Ray Ogden created these sinister other
worlds as well as their highly imaginative grotesque inhabi-
tants, often directly inspired by natural history books.

The most effective way to combine the two elements of live
actors and animation, was by the use of colour separation
overlay. CSO is an electronic process whereby the camera

Background and foreground card captions for composite picture.

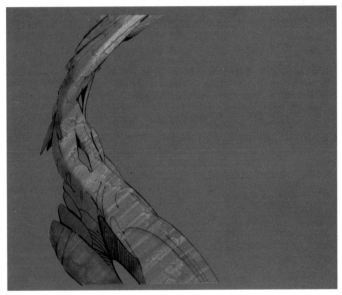

records everything except a particular colour, in this case blue. The actors work in an empty, blue studio, the colour being replaced electronically by one of the graphic illustrations on a rostrum stand some distance away.

These card captions provide the background and foreground of the on-screen picture. The system becomes more complicated as more layers of 'scenery' are required. Pilkington likens this build-up to a child's pop-up book.

'We are always trying to create an impression of depth rather than a flat presentation,' he says. 'The greatest number of layers we've had was six.'

'Using actors in drawings has been done before,' says Pilkington, 'but where we've broken new ground is that we have actors talking to the drawings. This meant that Ray had to devise a way that would not seem strange for his characters which don't have mouths to talk to Captain Zep.'

But equally a way had to be devised for the actor, who was speaking to the drawn character, to know where it was!

'It's a very difficult exercise talking to nothing,' says Pilkington. 'Eye-lines are the secret of all CSO work. I had a

very long blue pole with a blue disc on it which could be moved up and down, placed in the studio for each actor. This was a very quick way of getting the right eye-line.'

The other essential for good CSO work is lighting and here Pilkington worked with two masters of the art, Dave Jervis, the Electronics Effects Operator and the lighting man Bert Posthlethwaite.

'Bert knows just how to light for CSO,' says Pilkington. 'This has a lot to do with creating and removing shadows. Dave has an electronic box of tricks which he operates in collaboration with Bert. He ensured that special electronic processing was incorporated to reduce one of the most common problems of "fringing".'

Modern technology was also used to turn the human voice and the sound-track of *Captain Zep* into science fiction. All 180 drawn characters were played by three radio actors. Sound supervisor Anthony Philpot dehumanised them with the help of graphic equalisers and harmonisers, while Dick Mills from the BBC's radiophonic workshop used a synthesiser for the sound effects.

Ben (Jason Brown) being positioned by floor manager Geoff Walmsley. Blue poles indicate sight lines.

Composite picture of Ben and clawed monster.

Foreground and (*right*) background artwork of claws.

Final mix (*top*), background (*centre*), foreground (*below*).

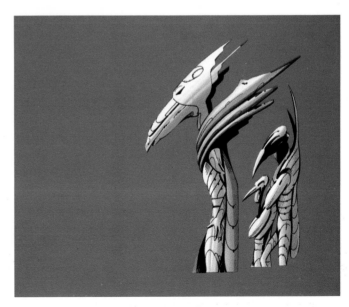

Raising The Rose

Prince Charles preparing to dive, surrounded by, among others, *Mary Rose* divers and the *Chronicle* team.
Below: Bob Everitt with his hand-held camera 150ft up in the crow's nest on *Tog Mor.*

King Henry VIII's flagship the *Mary Rose* had slumbered beneath the seas of the Solent for four centuries so another day made no difference to her. But for outside broadcast producer Roy Davies that Sunday when nothing was happening seemed almost as long as those 400 years.

'It contained all the classic elements of every OB producer's nightmare—having time to fill and nothing to fill it with,' explains Davies. 'On the Sunday we had a 40-minute highlights programme on what hadn't happened!'

The 24-hour delay occurred because one of the legs of the lifting frame supporting the *Mary Rose* had been unaccountably bent. The most noteworthy event that day was Prince Charles, patron of the Mary Rose Trust, disappearing from view underwater in diving gear to inspect the damage.

During the six months' planning for this historic broadcast, there were always contingency plans in case the weather on the appointed day was bad. Ironically, on the chosen day the conditions were perfect. The brilliant sunshine and calm sea attracted a colourful flotilla of yachts and would have turned the occasion into a vivid pageant, a suitable welcome for such an important Royal arrival. 'On the Monday the weather was utterly atrocious,' says Davies, 'and, of course, all the boats had gone.'

But if that Sunday held agonies of anxiety about the content of the on-screen presentation, behind the scenes the BBC was about to play a vital, if unexpected, role in lifting the *Rose*.

Over the last ten years, *Chronicle*, the BBC's archaeology and history unit whose team was responsible for this OB, has

Previous pages: OB cameraman Derek Wright ending his two days on the colour roving eye, positioned on a catamaran.

Moments after the lifting frame collapsed, Prince Charles (in light coat) inspected the damage.

been dedicated to the raising of the *Rose*. Programmes about the project, at the behest of first the executive producer, the late Paul Johnstone, and the current editor Bruce Norman, have done much to create the great public interest and enthusiasm for this remarkable salvage operation. However, it was never envisaged that the BBC might put its own technology to the task as well—something which, of course, everyone was only too happy to do.

It looked disastrous when the leg bent because it prevented the perfect docking operation with the Mary Rose Trust's sonar equipment. One of the BBC's most spectacular views was an aerial shot from the hand-held camera of Bob Everitt 150ft up in the crow's nest on *Tog Mor*, the floating crane, one of the biggest in the world.

'Margaret Rule, the Archaeological Director of the Mary Rose Trust, asked us if we could leave the shot on their monitor,' says Davies, 'so we left it locked off which enabled them to position the frame over the cradle from our pictures. They needed the picture for their attempt to dock it visually.' This meant an extra couple of hours' work for Everitt. 'The physical difficulties were immense for him,' says Davies. 'He refused to come in for lunch or for any physical comfort so he was there on Sunday and Monday from 5.30 am to 6 pm.'

There was only one hour when the doughty Mr Everitt left his exposed, uncomfortable eyrie, made even worse by Monday's driving rain. Water had got into his camera. Technicians took it apart and dried it and within an hour he was back on top of it all.

Altogether 11 cameras were used for the project. Six covered the main commentary position with Clare Francis at Southsea Castle and the procession of the *Mary Rose* down the Solent, and five were concentrated around the spot where she finally emerged.

Apart from the bird's-eye view on *Tog Mor*, there was another on board *Tog Mor*'s observation deck where an equally resilient trouper, reporter Bruce Parker from BBC Southampton, established something of a record himself by being on air that Monday from 7.55 in the morning to 3.30 in the afternoon. He broke for only half an hour. In this time he stripped off his rain-sodden clothes—shoes and all—placed them in *Tog Mor*'s tumble drier and 30 minutes later was again in front of the cameras a drier and happier man.

Two cameras were on *Sleipner*, the former Navy salvage vessel which was bought by the Mary Rose Trust. Aboard was co-producer John Selwyn Gilbert whose dedication to the whole *Mary Rose* venture led him to learn to dive in order to make films about it. His vast knowledge of the project made him the ideal person to interview Margaret Rule who was directing operations from *Sleipner*.

Finally, the fifth camera, the Colour Roving Eye on top of a Citroën Safari estate car, usually used at the races, was bobbing about on a catamaran much to the discomfort of cameraman Derek Wright who had to cope with an additional hazard. Apart from the long, tedious hours in the cold and wet when he described this job as being 'about as exciting as watching paint dry', he had to avoid being seasick.

The Aerodrome

Richard Johnson (Air Vice-Marshal) in the make-up room.

Between takes, actors shelter from the rain.

Actor Peter Firth having his make-up repaired.

Rex Warner's book *The Aerodrome* was published in 1941 but written before the start of the Second World War. It is the tale of the rise and brief triumph of a totalitarian state run by men who believed in a master race, defined by technological superiority. It is a story as appropriate now as it was prophetic then.

Warner chose an aerodrome as a futuristic symbol. He placed this closed, fanatical community of airmen in a requisitioned country house on a hill above a tranquil English village in the Cotswolds.

The producer, Kenith Trodd, whose name has been associated with some of the most innovative drama on television, notably Dennis Potter's *Pennies from Heaven*, had to convince today's audience that something as commonplace as an aerodrome could represent an evil, alien force.

He also had to clear from people's minds the debris of all those Second World War flying films which would have got in the way of the style and content of Warner's book.

'I was very determined to get rid of anything which reminded people of the last war,' says Trodd. 'The book is a vision of the future. It is a fantasy world created out of known elements plus the unknown exotic element of a master race. It is very introspective and retrospective.'

'We debated about trying to create very striking, unfamiliar and unacceptable kinds of pictures so that the look was strange.' Instead, Trodd and his team decided that a more dramatic device would be to set the story in the familiar, reassuring setting of rural England so that the sinister and bizarre message of the book would emerge with the greatest possible impact.

Trodd set his film in the mid-thirties when a 1950s jet aircraft would have looked futuristic.

This meant that the production had to assemble its own air force which, in the end, totalled nine planes. The two flying T-33 Shooting Stars and one flying Vampire were in private hands. The flying Vulcan, of the type which bombed Stanley Airport in the Falklands conflict, was courtesy of the Royal Air Force. It has since become one of the more popular exhibits at the Imperial War Museum at Duxford where much of the filming was done.

Four of the non-flying airoplanes of the 'Aerodrome' force were also found there—two Gloucester Meteors, early Fifties twin-engine bombers; a Vampire and the original test prototype of Concorde which is quite unlike the commercial version. It has no seats and is full of high technology instrumentation and test equipment. The final member of this air force was another Vulcan. It was used by RAF Catterick for fire practice and Trodd's team were allowed to film this.

The Air Vice-Marshal, played by Richard Johnson, boards a grounded Vulcan bomber at the Imperial War Museum. When he is seen sitting down, he is actually sitting in the test prototype of Concorde. Then we cut to a Vulcan taking off and finally he is 'seen' being blown-up in the Vulcan which was used for fire practice at Catterick.

Opposite: Night shoot at the Imperial War Museum, Duxford. The lighting was specially rigged for the occasion.

The Paras

Glyn Worsnip interviewing a parachutist with cameraman Dave Gray and sound recordist Mervyn Broadway.

At 7 am on January 11, 1982, 41 recruits arrived at Aldershot Station in Hampshire for an intensive 22-week training course, said to be one of the most gruelling in the world, for induction into the Parachute Regiment.

Producer/director Bill Jones planned an early night the evening before to be fresh and ready for the start of what he believed would be one of his most arduous assignments. What he did not realise was that even before he began, he would be confronted with the kind of obstacle which would make an assault course seem like an easy run.

At 10 pm on January 10, an official from the Ministry of Defence who had arrived in Aldershot an hour earlier, told Jones he could not start filming unless he complied with certain conditions.

'These would have made a nonsense of the whole ethos and idea of the series,' says Jones.

What was particularly surprising about this was that David Harrison, the executive producer of the series, had negotiated at length with the Parachute Regiment and the Ministry of Defence over the previous six months, and both had agreed to the series.

'We had to get David out of his bed in London and bring him down to a hotel in Aldershot and eventually by 4 am a compromise was reached,' says Jones. 'That was that a minder would stay with us. As it turned out, he decided to leave after a couple of weeks.'

Once this 'little local difficulty' had been settled, Jones and his team reporter Glyn Worsnip, the cameraman Dave Gray and the sound recordist, Mervyn Broadway, could get on with the job they were there to do.

'We went in with no preconceived idea other than to show what it was like to join up in the Paras,' says Jones. 'I knew they did a lot of intensive physical and mental activity and my intention was to be there when the important moments happened. To show the high spots which might have been the low spots, when the boys broke down, for example. But equally, we wanted to be on the spot to show them when they achieved something they were proud of.'

'Before we started I said to every lad individually that we would be filming them and that that meant the bad times as well as the good,' he continues. 'I asked them to tell us if they didn't want to appear and we wouldn't feature them. A couple did, so we didn't show them.'

The team had to be quick on their feet because there was no question of a re-take.

'If we had missed something it would have been our fault and hard luck,' says Jones, 'but I'm pleased to say we never did.'

After 12 weeks' training, the recruits take part in a three-day route march to discover which of them have the resolution and stamina for parachute training.

'They are pushed through the pain barrier,' says Jones, 'just to see who can tolerate it.'

'I walked the ten-mile route three times trying to imagine if I were a Para with a 40lb pack on my back and carrying a rifle, being hurried along, where I would crack, where I would say "enough",' he explains. 'I put camera crews at exactly the nine positions along the course I thought this would happen and it worked.'

Not that the crews simulated the Paras' tough transit across country because they travelled from site to site in Range Rovers.

Prince Charles, Colonel-in-Chief of the Parachute Regiment, at their Falklands Memorial Service.
Below: Filming the passing out parade of the 480 platoon on the drill square at Aldershot.

Opposite: Paras on one of their gruelling training courses, and (*inset*) a successful landing.

David Jones, the distinguished Royal Shakespeare Director, saw his production as an Elizabethan documentary.

'*The Merry Wives of Windsor* is the most documented play that Shakespeare wrote,' he says, 'with the possible exception of *Henry the Eighth*. It is full of eccentric characters but they are very much part of the small-town Shakespearean world. Everything about the play is Elizabethan so it is firmly rooted in 1600.'

The social comment comes through the two families, the *nouveaux riches* Fords (Ben Kingsley and Judy Davis) and the more established Pages (Bryan Marshall and Prunella Scales). A further social dimension is added by Fenton (Simon Chandler), an aristocratic young man who courts Anne Page (Miranda Foster).

Emphasising the realistic presentation of this jolly autumnal romp between two rich married women and that charming impecunious old rogue Falstaff (Richard Griffiths), is the costume design.

'As this was an everyday story of Elizabethan folk,' says costume designer Christine Rawlins, 'the costumes had to be real and not stylised.' For practical reasons, she modified the wide farthingales, those hooped skirts worn by the 'Merry Wives'. 'Prunella and Judy had to rush about a great deal, doing things like pushing people into baskets,' says Christine, 'so we cut their wide skirts down. Also, the sets were not particularly large and they would have been bumping into each other.'

That was the only concession she made to the small screen and the twentieth century. She found the prototype for most of the main characters' costumes in contemporary paintings.

The enchanting miniature painting of a young nobleman by Nicholas Hilliard, in the Victoria and Albert Museum, was the basis for Fenton's costume.

Elizabeth Spriggs, who plays Mistress Quickly, wears a beautiful gold embroidered gown in the final moonlit scene in Windsor Park. It is a scene of revelry and magic in which Mistress Quickly is cast as the Fairy Queen. Christine based this costume on a gown worn by Queen Elizabeth I in a picture known as the Ditchley Portrait, in the National Portrait Gallery. She found an old bit of curtain fabric which she says was 'a bit brassy and shiny, but it was vaguely an Elizabethan design that we could work on. It was also light in colour and weight, so we could play with it and put bits on.'

'Since materials are very difficult to get, you look for the fabrics first and the ideas come later,' she says.

To suggest the new money of the Fords she added fussy, unnecessary pieces of fur to Judy Davis's costume and gave her an extra coat which was not really needed.

From Christine's point of view, an extra bonus in the casting of Richard Griffiths as Falstaff was his size. 'It was marvellous not having to pad him,' she says. 'Padding never looks as convincing, and it's terribly hot for the actor as well as rather uncomfortable.'

When the costumes are finished it's not the end of the job. They are sprayed to take off the surface newness. 'Television tends to prettify everything,' says Christine, 'and I didn't want the clothes to look as if they had just come from the makers, which they had.'

David Jones says the secret of successful costume design is a three-way partnership between designer, actor and director right from the start, so that everyone is very clear about what is wanted.

'In television you have to trust your designer much more than in the theatre,' he says.

BBC Television Shakespeare: The Merry Wives of Windsor

Costume fittings for Elizabeth Spriggs (Mistress Quickly) and with costume designer Christine Rawlins.

Windsor Great Park recreated in Studio One.

Left to right: Alan Bennett (Justice Shallow), Ben Kingsley (Ford), Richard Griffiths (Falstaff), Prunella Scales (Mistress Page).

Elizabeth Spriggs playing the Fairy Queen wearing a gown inspired by the Ditchley Portrait of Elizabeth I.

Director David Jones with Prunella Scales and Richard Griffiths.

'Merry Wives' Judy Davis (Mistress Ford) and Prunella Scales.

113

BBC transportable satellite terminal at Kingswood Warren where it was constructed.

Living in the future is a fact of life for the 80 BBC boffins of the Engineering Research Department.

But while these engineers and scientists invent and develop the technology which will take the BBC into the twenty-first century, they work in an environment of Victorian calm and oak-panelled splendour at Kingswood Warren. This 150-year-old mansion, 20 miles from London, is set in 30 acres of lawns and woods in North Surrey.

'Things that happen here might take five to ten years before they are out in the market-place if they are going into the public domain,' says Dr Bruce Moffat, Head of the Studio Group. 'If they are going into Television Centre, then between one and two years.'

His group's latest invention, an animation store associated with an electronic rostrum camera, is likely to revolutionise the art of animation. It was developed at the behest of the Graphics Department who has just taken delivery of it.

The Engineering Research Department works for BBC television, radio and the external services. It does research on everything from the microphone and camera, to optical devices, digital technique, signal processing, transmission systems, acoustics, aerials and propagation. The three services bring to the Department's attention any technical trends they wish to have developed but it also originates much of its own research. The work is very much applied research with a practical use to everything that is done.

Three Queen's Awards for Industry have been won by BBC engineering. The Kingswood Warren team were honoured for their work on techniques for the conversion of television pictures from the American 525 line standard to the European 625 lines, and Teletext, for which they did most of the development work.

A recent piece of new technology is the mobile satellite link equipment. It consists of a three-metre-wide aerial 'dish' on a small trailer. It has been in use for two years and was part of the BBC's OB transmitting facilities from Spain during the World Cup.

In 1986 the BBC will begin direct broadcasting by satellite. The satellite, hovering 22,000 miles above Brazil, will provide two new network channels for the BBC—DBS1 and 2. Part of the essential equipment for receiving these programmes will be a one-metre 'dish' aerial.

The BBC is developing its own aerial receiver, a flat panel which has an array of button receptors. This, the scientists and engineers of Kingswood Warren believe, will be a vast improvement on the unsightly 'dish'.

'Satellite transmission is technically the nearest to the ideal of a true broadcasting system that we have ever had,' says Dr Geoffrey Phillips, Head of the Radio Frequency Group, and an expert on satellite systems. 'You need to have only one transmitter of 200 watts which can reach the whole of the United Kingdom.'

And what of the future these men inhabit daily? The groundwork is being done on high definition television to give four times as much detail as we now have. Within the next ten years, we should be able to have a six-foot by four-foot picture using more than 1000 lines. Scientists who have seen this in the laboratory describe the results as breathtaking. And, according to Dr Moffat, we will be able to make our televisions think for us. 'At present you programme your video to record future programmes,' he says. 'In the Nineties, it should be possible to set your television to take account of any changes or delays in a programme's showing. In other words, put a brain in your television.'

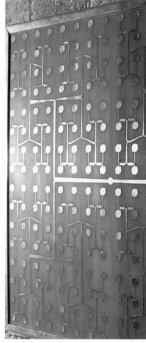

Above: Close-up of panel aerial of the future.

116

Receiving aerials for home reception of direct broadcasts from a satellite.
Top: Using current technology, and (bottom) panel under development.

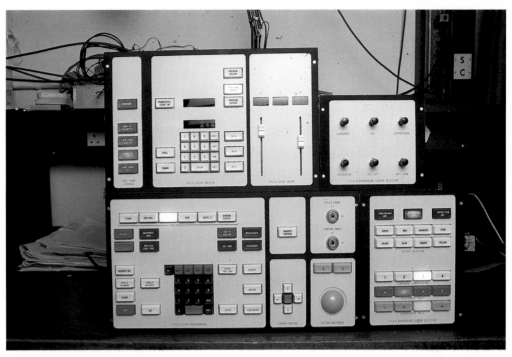

Above: The control panels of the system in the laboratory during final development; sequence programming, previewing, vision mixing and overlay facilities are provided.
Below left: The magnetic disc-pack multi-picture store.

The television rostrum camera which is the main source of picture signals for storing and elaborate processing in the system.

117

Warm-up man Jimmy Perry keeping the audience happy and (*below*) Terry Wogan shows
a leg for charity, much to the amusement of singing stars Lulu and Petula Clark.

The first radio studio set up inside a television studio. In the foreground (left to right)
Terry Wogan, Paul Daniels, Lulu, Petula Clark, Cliff Richard, Henry Cooper and James Hunt.

'We were about to start seven hours of transmission and nobody could find Cardiff,' says director Pieter Morpurgo, speaking about the 1981 edition of the programme, which opened with a contribution from each of the major BBC regional stations.

'This wasn't Cardiff's fault. Bristol had finished *Nationwide* and then switched off its link with us in London and gone to tea,' he continues. 'Cardiff comes through the Bristol switching centre. We only got Cardiff ten seconds before transmission. There were a lot of shaky, white-faced people about and I was one of them. I aged ten years. I am glad to say nothing like that happened in 1982.'

This marathon charity appeal which in 1982 raised well over one million pounds, made use of the combined forces of BBC television, radio and local radio. For the first time in 1982 there was a radio studio working independently inside a television studio.

'It's the sort of thing I adore doing,' says Morpurgo, 'because technically it is extremely complicated. It is probably as complicated as any other television programme, including the General Election. In effect you are running the whole BBC1 network for the night.'

There were cameras at work in every BBC television station in the country. These included the national regions, the network production centres and local television studios which total 17. There were also three outside broadcasts at Radio Sheffield, Radio Northampton and Radio Medway. Altogether 65 cameras were used, some for the network and some for their particular areas, and 11 producers and 11 directors worked outside London.

At Television Centre, Morpurgo worked with the executive producer Mark Patterson who was responsible for the overall editorial shape of the programme, regional editor Mike Read who collated all the stories from the regions, radio co-ordinator Mike Gilliam and producer Hugh Purcell who looked after the stories sent in by phone.

But Morpurgo believes the man who really carried the programme was presenter Terry Wogan. 'It lives or dies on Terry,' he says.

The programme went on the air at 6.55 pm and the first five minutes were scripted, but after that 'it meant making it up as you went along,' says Morpurgo.'

It is the kind of operation which brings out the very best in people who gladly volunteer their services. From those manning the telephones to celebrities who come in to the studio, they all willingly give up their time to work on it.

Temporary telephone exchanges sprang up in the most unlikely places. One was to be found on the *Saturday Superstore* set, another in the make-up room at Lime Grove's Topical Presentation Unit.

Throughout the night there was a relay of information with stories coming in from London and the regions. When these were collated, 'runners' took them to Terry or Fran Morrison on the news desk or gave them to one of the celebrities.

Terry could also be alerted through his earpiece that a story was coming from one of the regions.

'Really my job was that of a co-ordinator because I rely on everybody knowing their job without having to be told,' says Morpurgo. 'To get it right you must have the co-operation of everyone concerned. It's an unusual sort of one-off event and we still get very excited about it. We all love doing things which stretch us, where we can use our inventive talents.'

Throughout the evening, recorded items are inserted into the programme from the videotape
area at Television Centre. *Below:* A VT engineer with a machine that placed the items into the network.

Volunteers man the telephones collecting pledges from callers (*below left*). The *Saturday Superstore* set in Studio Seven (*above and below right*) became one of the temporary telephone exchanges.

Two Ronnies Christmas Show

A fifteenth-century manor house becomes the two Ronnies' home for a day

Below: The 'props' for a coach gag arrive.

The two Ronnies have been dropping clangers to great comic effect on screen for years but there would have been little to laugh at if they had dropped one now. They were in the depths of the Surrey countryside dressed as ice-cream sellers with shiny brass bells tied round their ankles but when the time came to record the sketch they found themselves up a lane without a cart. We hadn't noticed that props had gone on ahead with the ice-cream cart and left the boys 100 yards up the road,' says producer Paul Jackson.

Stage manager Peter March and assistant floor manager Neil Banks smartly lifted up Ronnie Corbett and carried him to the cart, but there was no suggestion that the same thing would happen to Ronnie Barker. He was left to accompany himself on bells as he made his way very carefully down the road. The bells, after all, had been generously if somewhat foolhardily lent to them by the company of bell-ringers appearing on the show. But they need not have worried. Ronnie Barker rarely puts a foot wrong.

Any programme starring the two Ronnies—and particularly their Christmas special—is eagerly awaited. Not only are their shows hilarious, mostly written by one of the funniest men in the business, Gerald Wiley alias Ronnie Barker, but a popular feature has become the fulsomely staged production number. Christmas 1982 was no exception.

Paul Jackson asked his production assistant Tony Newman to find a picturesque manor house, accessible to London and not on a flight path. He went to the seventh floor of Television Centre to the BBC Locations Index. This contains files and photographs of 30,000 locations in Britain which have been either used in the past by the BBC or brought to their notice by people sending in information.

'We can supply details on anything from an abattoir to a weather station,' says Robert Ashburn, Facilities Manager. 'The biggest section is House and Garden which is split into period and county,' he continues. The BBC is soon to purchase a micro-processor to increase the amount of information instantly available. Ashburn estimates there are about 5000 locations used by the BBC annually, of which 500 become new files. 'There is no comparable facilities unit elsewhere in British television as no other TV company is big enough to support it,' says Ashburn.

Old Surrey Hall in East Grinstead, a fifteenth-century manor house and the home of West End solicitor Cyril Alfille, was selected as the most suitable place for the two Ronnies to shoot four-and-a-half minutes of gags about bells.

For a day Mr Alfille and his beautiful house with its ornamental lake and vast grounds were host to a production team of 60, sundry bell-ringers, a coach and four horses and a 19-ton outside broadcast van. To everyone's credit, when it was over he was still able to smile and say: 'I didn't mind.'

The *Two Ronnies* regularly makes extensive use of the wide range of facilities which the BBC can offer. It could be the Pronunciation Unit, Special Effects or even one of the foreign language units. The shows are also a happy blend of film, videotape and studio recording.

These days film is used less often and Jackson says they only have it for the Piggy Malone-type serials. It is more time-consuming than VT as it has to be set up shot by shot, processed and then edited, whereas video leapfrogs these stages allowing the producer the great luxury of seeing immediately what has been shot. This is particularly valuable when doing comedy. 'You're not quite as concerned as you are in drama about the creation of a mood,' says Jackson. 'What you want to know is whether the joke has come off.'

123

Ronnie Barker doing a bell hop.

Ronnie Corbett being carried by stage manager Peter March (right) and Neil Banks, assistant floor manager.

Snooker: The Coral UK Championship

Terry Griffiths watching his opponent Alex Higgins
on the last day of the 1982 Championship in Preston.

For an ever-growing number of people there is more drama in the fate of 22 coloured balls than in the most lurid television soap opera. In fact, in 1980 when a black ball was trapped in the jaws of a pocket with only two reds left, Willie Thorne and Bill Werbeniuk spent 25 minutes playing tactics without potting a ball. The public loved it and deluged the BBC with letters and telephone calls to say so.

In 1981 snooker attracted 15.5 million viewers and in 1982 it reached 18 million with 88 hours of viewing time.

Pot Black began in 1969. Colour television meant snooker was much more easily understood and its popularity increased. The studio-based *Pot Black* whetted the public's appetite for the dramatic tension of the World Championship, now held in the Crucible Theatre, Sheffield.

The next major step in the popularisation of the game by television came in 1977. 'We were to televise the last few frames of the 1976 World Championship,' says producer Nick Hunter. 'I went along to watch the game and was amazed at what was happening. Higgins was doing death-defying acts and in each match coming back from nowhere to win it. There was no build up to our coverage. Our frames tended to be rather academic and not very exciting. I thought we ought to be doing more.'

There was doubt, however, whether snooker could maintain an audience every day of the week during a championship. But an even more serious handicap had to be solved before the real breakthrough in the game's popularity—the problem of the television lights. This happened after an argument at the 1976 World Championship.

'We lit the table and the players didn't like it,' says Hunter. 126 'I wanted to get the players over to the public. I wanted to

The commentary position overlooking the main auditorium.

The two scoring officials in the foreground
watch Griffiths, the eventual winner.

show Higgins about to play a shot or show John Spencer reacting after he had missed one. Before 1976 there were not many close-ups of the players, they used to disappear into the darkness because of the way the lighting was arranged.'

Every light source over the table gives a reflection on the snooker ball so with 40 lamps over and around the table, there are 40 reflections on each of the 22 balls.

John Crowther, the engineering manager in Manchester, Mike Watterson, the tournament promoter who represented the players' interests and Hunter went into the studio to work out how to light around the table without worrying the players. 'A kind of skirt was devised to shield the snooker balls from the lamps.'

'In 1978 Aubrey Singer, then Controller of BBC2, agreed to take the World Championship every day and that was the year everyone began to realise there was something in this game.'

A year later they solved their last problem. Strip-lighting was used instead of individual lamps. They are much cooler and do not explode but flicker when they need renewing. 'In the space of three years we completely altered the light on the table,' Hunter continues, 'and I think that has had a lot to do with the success of snooker on television because the players were more comfortable with the lighting which improved their performance.'

'We try to give the impression of the mood and tension of the place,' he says, 'but we don't go in for gimmicks like split screens and we don't move our cameras during a championship to try to improve an angle. The best compliment we can have is that the players forget we are there.'

127

Actors Nigel Hawthorne (Sir Humphrey Appleby), Derek Fowlds (Bernard Woolley) and Paul Eddington (Cabinet Minister James Hacker) at the BBC rehearsal rooms, Acton. *Below:* Same scene in the studio.

Yes Minister

Producer Peter Whitmore rehearsing lines with Paul Eddington.

Yes Minister is avidly watched both in Westminster and Whitehall but whether the politicians and the civil servants look at it to laugh or to learn is not recorded. What *is* known is that the show is even more accurate than some Ministers are aware. 'A former Minister criticised the way a Cabinet Secretary had dealt with Sir Humphrey,' says producer Peter Whitmore, 'and when the writers [Jonathan Lynn and Anthony Jay] queried this with someone from the civil service side he said it could well have happened. The writer had got a little nearer to the truth than the Minister realised.'

Lynn and Jay never reveal their sources—not even to Whitmore—but have acknowledged that help has come from those at the top. 'I make a great point of not trying to know because if I start treating it as a documentary we might lose our way,' says Whitmore. 'We have got to remember we are there to make people laugh. It is basically a comedy.'

Nevertheless, every effort is made to ensure that it all looks as authentic as possible. Special stationery for the fictional Ministry of Administrative Affairs is printed and the red despatch boxes used are made by the same company which makes them for the Government. The set designers studied a BBC documentary which filmed Margaret Thatcher in her office at the House of Commons.

Producing such a highly successful comedy is no laughing matter for the actors who include Paul Eddington as Cabinet Minister James Hacker, Nigel Hawthorne as Sir Humphrey Appleby, that consummate civil servant, and Derek Fowlds as Hacker's Private Secretary. They have an intense seven-day-a-week schedule for seven weeks. 'A lot of the week is very hard work and tremendous concentration is needed to remember the script and you don't break that by giggling too much,' says

Whitmore. 'These are actors who are brilliant at comedy rather than comedians like Dave Allen or Les Dawson who instinctively go out of their way to make people laugh.'

Every Monday morning they meet at 10.30 at the BBC rehearsal rooms in North Acton, known in the trade as the Acton Hilton. There are 18 rehearsal rooms in this bleak, 13-year-old, 7-floor, purpose-built block which look more like abandoned National Health wards than a small-screen fun-factory where some of the world's finest television begins life. 'It's bare and clinical for obvious reasons,' says Whitmore. 'We know what it's going to be like, an actor gets conditioned to that.'

The writers attend the first read-through on Monday and any queries the actors have about dialogue are settled then. They work until two each day without a lunch break and then go home to work on their lines. There is no call on Tuesday so by 10 am on Wednesday the actors can rehearse without scripts. On Friday the writers return and at noon there is a technical run-through with the lighting, sound, design, costume and make-up people. 'We are still at Acton on Saturday,' continues Whitmore, who was responsible for the second and third series, and who, like the show's first producer Sydney Lotterby, has won a BAFTA award for *Yes Minister*. 'We do a couple of run-throughs, polishing, polishing all the time.' On Sunday they go into the studio at Television Centre and work from 10.30 to 1.30 with an hour for lunch, then the dress rehearsal at 2.30 with perhaps another run-through at 5 followed by a supper break. The show is recorded between 8 and 9.30 that night before a studio audience, and 13 hours later they are all together once more at Acton to start the process all over again.

Rehearsing a scene in Hacker's living room. The poles indicate doors or corners of the set.
Below: Peter Whitmore (top left) giving notes to the cast after the Sunday afternoon camera rehearsal.

Brian Jones, production manager doing the audience warm-up.

The Queen's theme for her broadcast in 1982 was the important role the sea has played in the life of Britain and the Commonwealth. But what the 50 million viewers around the world did not know was that while she was speaking of the sea, the sky was playing an important if totally unhelpful role in her own life.

For the first time the broadcast was recorded at Windsor Castle—in the Library. This meant that every minute or so, aircraft from nearby Heathrow Airport were heard overhead.

Usually The Queen's Christmas message is between five and six minutes long and filmed in segments. This time there had to be more interruptions due to the noise but, ironically, it made the occasion even more relaxed.

'We were all up against a common enemy,' says producer Richard Cawston who made the memorable 1969 television film *Royal Family* and has subsequently produced every Christmas broadcast since 1970.

If pets grow to be like their owners, so some producers become like their productions. Cawston is a tall, distinguished man, silver-tongued and silver-haired, regal in style and commanding in presence.

Cawston emphasises that this is not a BBC programme but one which the corporation has traditionally produced for the monarch each year.

The Christmas message for television and a separate one for radio (in stereo) are recorded in a couple of hours one morning during the first half of December. The content of the text is The Queen's and she works on this intensively throughout November. The broadcast has to be done in advance to make sure it arrives at some of the remoter parts of the Commonwealth in time for Christmas. One year it was done too late and did not get to the Christmas Islands in time!

It is a straightforward film-making operation made as relaxed as possible by Richard Cawston and his team of ten. The Queen appears to be very much at ease with them all, no doubt because the key members of the team worked on *Royal Family* and have been involved in every Christmas broadcast since. And obviously she has become very knowledgeable about the techniques of film-making over the years.

'I usually do two takes of everything in case the film is damaged, which fortunately it never has been,' says Cawston.

Things were very different before 1969 when the Christmas message was done as a full-scale outside broadcast with trucks in the gardens of Buckingham Palace, cables running through the corridors and sometimes eight times as many people as Cawston uses, turning up at the Palace.

Opposite: The Queen and producer Richard Cawston looking at some of the prints of old sailing ships used in her 1982 broadcast. This was filmed in the Library of Windsor Castle for the first time. The picture also shows production assistant Ann Hewitt and assistant cameraman Philip Sindall.

Left: The Queen, her Private Secretary Sir Philip Moore (back right) and the BBC production team which included Richard Cawston, cameraman Philip Bonham-Carter, his assistant Philip Sindall, sound recordist Terry Elms, his assistant Les Honess and film lighting men David Gorringe and Derek Stockley.

Royal Family changed all that. It broke new ground because it used modern, intimate film techniques in the presence of Royalty, something which had not been done before. Without any loss of dignity, the Royal Family were heard speaking informally to each other just like any other family. The success of these techniques changed the face of Royalty forever and convinced The Queen that this was the way to do her Christmas broadcasts.

Nowadays, the number of BBC people in the same room as The Queen is kept to a minimum with never more than eight. Last year they included Richard Cawston, production assistant Ann Hewitt, cameraman Philip Bonham-Carter who uses one 16mm lightweight camera and his assistant Philip Sindall, sound man Terry Elms and his assistant Les Honess, and film lighting men David Gorringe and Derek Stockley.

When The Queen's message was recorded in the Regency Room at Buckingham Palace, where it was done for a number of years, the two Autocue operators and three extra electricians were stationed in the bathroom next door to be out of sight and to keep the numbers down.

The Queen has her hair done by her own hairdresser and she does her own make-up but often discusses with Cawston the colour of the dress she will wear or whether a diamond brooch

will be too bright for the camera. The final choice is hers, however.

The entire broadcast, like the message itself, is of no fixed length and can be less than five minutes or over 20. During the last 13 years, the nature of the broadcast has changed, sometimes substantially. Apart from a filmed title sequence—two have been from a helicopter of The Queen's Flight—it includes footage specially filmed during the year and planning for this begins in January.

In 1971, for example, the two young Princes, Andrew and Edward, were seen sitting on a sofa with The Queen, discussing a family photograph album.

At Princess Anne's wedding two years later, Cawston's crew was the only one allowed to film behind the scenes in the Balcony Room of Buckingham Palace.

And, when appropriate, the crew travels abroad with the Royal party. In 1970 they were aboard the Royal yacht *Britannia* sailing into Botany Bay, Australia—a privilege no other film crew has enjoyed. Also that year, they filmed The Queen at Yellowknife in Canada.

Amid all the new people she meets, it must be a comfort for The Queen to see the same familiar faces turning up year after year all over the world.

Weatherman Jim Bacon giving a lunchtime weather report from a small presentation studio at Television Centre.
Below: Resting magnetic isobars.

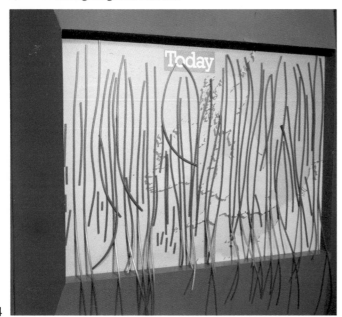

'When you wake up after a late night shift and ask your wife "what time did the rain start?" it's like getting the results of a crossword,' says Jim Bacon, one of the BBC's weathermen. Jim Bacon loves our weather. But what he likes even more is talking about it. 'When there's a big depression in the Mediterranean or a low over Sweden you are bursting to tell people about it,' he says.

The weather segment of the news is part of the slack in the system. The BBC's weathermen who include Michael Fish and Bill Giles can either have 50 seconds or $1\frac{1}{2}$ minutes depending on whether a piece of film has arrived or not. When this happens Bacon says: 'It's bit like somebody giving you a Christmas present. We ad lib rather than read it off Autocue so it's not difficult to cope.'

'We've been digesting this stuff all day and there is always far more detail in the weather than we are able to put in. If we're given more time, it enables us to enjoy ourselves a little bit. Every weatherman is the same. You really have to put a bag over his head to stop him.'

Jim Bacon comes from Feltwell in Norfolk and grew up in the Fen district which he says is like being at sea—'there's an

Jim Bacon in his office compiling his weather report from overnight satellite charts.

The magnetic isobars being put into place half an hour before the lunchtime weather report.

The weatherman's filing cabinet for all seasons.

awful lot of sky'. He joined the Meteorological Office on leaving school and cannot think of a more interesting profession than weather forecasting. 'It is so exciting,' he says. 'It has so many different facets. If you think about our weather there is always something different going on from the previous day. It keeps you fresh. I count myself very lucky.'

'We are all weathermen first and presenters second,' says Bacon. 'We are part of the Met Office—we are the mouthpiece. We are not doing the forecasting all on our own. There are an awful lot of people behind the scenes whose work gives us the information we need to present our forecast, although our training enables us to interpret the charts and get a version ourselves. You will not get a forecast unless you have the analysis correct.'

Once Bacon had joined the Met he did a degree in meteorology at Reading University and it was while there that he was asked to audition as a BBC weatherman.

Bacon arrives at his small one-window office on the fifth floor of Television Centre at 10 in the morning. Two facsimile machines provide charts and satellite pictures of the whole of Europe transmitted overnight from the Met headquarters in Bracknell. This gives him a picture of the upper atmosphere. More information comes from commercial jets and radio sondes—small weather balloons. A plotted observation map of the British Isles with perhaps 100 pieces of detailed information gives Bacon the picture of British weather up to 12,000 feet.

He spends an hour in the morning doing the Atlantic chart which is the first one we see on our screens and 15 minutes each tracing the other two. Before every broadcast he confers with the senior forecasters at Bracknell and at the London Weather Centre in Holborn. Once all this mass of scientific information has been digested Bacon, like all the best trained weathermen, sticks his head out of the window to see what is happening.

'I often go on to the fire-escape just to get the feel of the weather,' he says. 'It can appear quite different from one side of a window to another.'

But if weather forecasting is a capricious business then coping with television weather props, like magnetic isobars, can be even more unpredictable. 'The trick is to get the right symbols in the right place and make sure they are not going to fall off,' he says.

Some of the thousands of Christmas cards received.

Twelve-foot teddy donated by Summerfield School, Bath.

'You live so much for the moment on a programme like this,' says Biddy Baxter, Editor of *Blue Peter*. She joined the programme as a producer in 1962 and became its Editor three years later when it went out twice weekly. In October 1983 it celebrated its 25th anniversary.

Every Monday and Thursday for ten months of the year, Biddy and her team take over one of the most spacious BBC studios at Television Centre, usually Studio One, the largest in Europe.

'We always use the biggest studio just so we can bring in the Red Army dancers or 200 pantomime horses,' says Biddy.

The night before a broadcast, the floor is painted white and the bare walls are covered by a white cyclorama or curtain. 'This is to make a light, bright, sparkling atmosphere,' says Biddy. High-key lighting using 250 lamps heightens the effect.

'I think the top priority for a long-running magazine show like this is unpredictability,' says Biddy. 'Children write in and say one of the reasons they like the show is because they never know what's going to happen next.'

But this element of unpredictability can sometimes get out of hand. On one occasion the studio was full of Girl Guides singing rousing action songs round a studio camp fire. 'To the astonishment of all of us in the gallery,' says Biddy, 'the flames leapt higher and higher with smoke billowing up in a dark cloud. Next thing, three BBC firemen with extinguishers leapt in and doused the flames'.

There is practically nothing that *Blue Peter* doesn't cover. 'Children are the most selective audience,' says Biddy; 'if they are bored they either switch off or switch over. We have such a wide age range, it's a very difficult discipline to appeal successfully to young and old alike. You don't want to talk down to them, but when you think of the mixed abilities of the audience you must do a lot of items on two levels. The little ones will appreciate the visuals and the older ones will take in the information.'

'It's the best audience in the world because they are so interested in what is going on and they are uncranky.' Seventy-five per cent of the ideas for the show are suggested by the children themselves. For their trouble they are awarded a *Blue Peter* badge. Once this happens, their names join the other hundreds of thousands on a card-index system in the show's special Correspondence Unit.

Every one of the 4000 letters received on average each week is read, and many confirm the popularity of items on how to make things.

'Being a live programme we can be topical,' says Biddy. So while the Americans and Russians were travelling into outer space in the beginning of 1983, the children of Britain were learning how to make a Planet Control Buggy out of a plastic ice-cream container, cotton reels and press-studs.

But the show is not all making toys from household scrap or watching the three presenters take part in hair-raising exploits. 'It looks life fair and square in the face,' says Biddy. 'We have shown such horrendous situations as starving children in Biafra, but it would be quite wrong to show this if you didn't tell the audience that they could do something to help: they do so through our *Blue Peter* appeals.

'We never ask for money,' says Biddy, 'the whole point of the appeals is to help the viewers as much as the good cause. We want to make contributing accessible to everyone no matter how badly off they are, so, in the past, viewers have partcipated by sending used stamps, old wool and cotton, silver paper or broken cutlery. Even with our Bring and Buy sale the bringers are as important as the buyers.'

Early morning preparations in Studio One for the Christmas show and (*below*) nine hours later
130 children singing carols, accompanied by the Chalk Farm Band of the Salvation Army.

Jim'll Fix It

Jane Wheeler (*above*) transformed into a $4\frac{1}{2}$-ft-tall gerbil by the costume department. *Top right:* Producer Roger Ordish (left), Jimmy Savile and director Peter Campbell teaching Jane how to act like a gerbil. Her efforts are rewarded (*right*) by the prized *Jim'll Fix It* badge.

The philosophy of Jimmy Savile OBE is simple. 'If you want anything spontaneous to happen,' he says, 'organise it.'

Each year 250,000 hopefuls write to Jimmy. These letters are sorted through by producer Roger Ordish, who has been with the show from its start in 1975, director Peter Campbell, two researchers and a secretary. Their strike rate is one in 5000.

Beside Roger Ordish in his sixth-floor office at Television Centre sits a large black plastic bag of lost causes. 'This is the "confidential waste" as it is called,' he says. 'We are always getting letters from boys who want to train with their favourite football team and girls wanting to ride with show-jumping stars,' says Ordish. 'And then pop music—you can date a letter by pop music.' The perfect formula he says should make the audience say 'Isn't she lucky, isn't she brave and isn't it funny.'

One suggestion which came very close to this was the bride whose sister asked Jim to organise an elephant ride for the happy couple from the church to the reception. Not only did the BBC's Special Effects Department build a howdah for the elephant's back on which the bridal couple was seated but Tom Fleming, the man who did the commentary for the Royal Wedding, was engaged for the occasion.

More recently, when nine-year-old Jane Wheeler wrote to Jim saying: 'Please could you fix it for me to dress up as a gerbil and run round and round on a wheel,' Roger knew he had found his one in 5000. A girl-sized kennel, wheel, polystyrene ball and furry gerbil suit were made up and Jane was soon in the studio being put through her paces by Jimmy.

The youngest person to appear on *Jim'll Fix It* was a three-year-old boy who wanted to do precision formation driving with earth-moving equipment, and when a mere lad of 104 asked to ride in a racing car, that too was arranged.

The show was the idea of Bill Cotton, then Controller of BBC1. Despite its great success in this country, it has failed elsewhere. Jimmy has no doubt why his show has always captured large audiences. For him the most important consideration is never to take advantage of anyone.

'I personally have a great horror of using people,' he says. 'I'd never tolerate that at any time. The success of my programme depends on not taking the mickey out of people for the sake of a cheap laugh. What we finish up with is something that participants can video as a souvenir and be proud of. That's why we've always been number one.'

'There are certain rules which I impose on the production team,' he continues, 'although of course Roger Ordish, my producer, chooses the letters. I won't have violence, lavatory humour or sexual innuendo—it is not a slot for that sort of thing.'

Jimmy has not forgotten himself in all the fixing that has been going on over the years. At 4 pm every studio afternoon he has tea served in his dressing-room on a silver salver, poured from a silver tea-pot and accompanied by cucumber sandwiches.

Film items are shot throughout the year for the 13-part series and incorporated into the programme which is recorded every Tuesday from the end of December for transmission the following Saturday week. The recording takes place in the newly decorated Shepherds Bush Television Theatre, previously the Shepherds Bush Empire, an old variety theatre. 'It is excellent from the audience's point of view,' says Ordish. 'And I rather like being there because you are away from Television Centre and it's your own ship whereas in the Centre you are just one of the programmes.'

Afternoon tea on a silver salver for Jim and (*below*) presenting a *Jim'll Fix It* badge.

139

Every Tuesday during its 13-week run, the show is recorded at the Television Theatre, Shepherds Bush, formerly a variety hall.
Below left: Jean Beaton threading some of the 104 badges awarded each year.

Frank Bough describes the first few weeks establishing *Breakfast Time* as 'like having jet lag without going anywhere,' but adds, 'it's not half as tiring when you are winning.'

At 6.30 am on Monday 17 January 1983 in the depths of the snowy, sleep-inducing midwinter, Bough, Selina Scott and Nick Ross made television history as the presenters of the first networked breakfast show in Europe. Pullover power had arrived.

The BBC in the person of Editor Ron Neil would appear to have got the breakfast formula right virtually from day one. 'I didn't want any desks,' he says, 'I wanted a relaxed feel to the show. People see the style of the programme now and they deliberately choose to wear a jumper or cardigan. It makes them feel relaxed too.' Neil who came to *Breakfast Time* from running *Newsnight* competed for the job at a BBC Board, one of those occasions when applicants are grilled by members of top management. They must seem like a court martial to the unsuccessful.

'It's the last new thing in television. There's nowhere else, from now on it's downhill,' jests 40-year-old Neil. 'The next highlight is the silver watch; no, it's the coronary.'

Neil, a tall, amiable Scot is not just well-liked by his team, he is much admired and respected by them. When *Breakfast Time* finished its first programme, a spontaneous burst of applause greeted his entry into the canteen.

He started work on May 11 which gave him just under eight months to assemble his forces. He whisked Selina away from ITN and placed her alongside Frank Bough, that steady old warhorse of live television's *Nationwide* and *Grandstand*. 'I thought Frank and Selina would be a combination which would not be an intrusion into your home but one which you would genuinely welcome,' he says. The mix was so successful they have become a sort of Burns and Allen double act of current affairs.

Others in the winning team include Nick Ross, the third presenter whose boyish smile belies his years of television experience and sharp brain. Francis Wilson has achieved the impossible and made talking about the weather sexy. David Icke's appealing face draws as many women as men to his sports slot, and Debbie Rix's approach to newscasting is authoritative rather than authoritarian. Astrologer Russell Grant enjoys being one of the stars as much as talking about them.

The other big advantage enjoyed by *Breakfast Time* is the BBC's huge news operation on which the team can draw.

But if the style and content of the show are as gentle and relaxing as the sprawling sofa they all recline on—even the lights are lower first thing in the morning—the technology which supports them is anything but lax. *Breakfast Time* is a 24-hour operation where one set of people has to hand over to another team. It thus demanded a different set of solutions from other live news and current affairs programmes.

Even before Ron Neil was appointed Editor, senior producer Tam Fry had been made special assistant and his job was to choose the high technology which would complement the low profile on screen. A Government grant of £25,000 provided the resources to purchase the Hewlett Packard computer equipment and some software which enabled the BBC Television Computer Services to develop a computerised newsroom system. It would have been extremely laborious to administer breakfast television in the usual fashion,' he explains. 'The computer takes away 25–30 per cent of the drudge.'

The computers are programmed with the running order, which consists of 100 items and means 120 pages of script, now typed by the computer. When a story is written it is automatically slotted into its place in the schedule. The computer also puts the script straight on to Autocue, which Neil claims happens nowhere else in the world. 'Normally it would take the director three hours to work out his running order in the traditional manner,' says Fry. 'This way takes 35 minutes and allows the human being more time.'

There are a hundred people working on *Breakfast Time* in London in a complicated series of shifts, which change every three days, to give a 24-hour coverage. It was essential, therefore, that the method of handing over from one team to another was as precise as possible.

When the presenters come in around 3.30 each morning they need only press a button on their visual display units to summon up all the information, placed in the computer by the overnight crew: all they need to know about the guests they are to interview that morning.

There are 40 terminals in the Newsroom but instead of the usual cheerful pandemonium and clattering of typewriters, the place hums quietly like a well-organised electronic beehive. 'The lack of noise is an unexpected boon,' says Fry. 'The extent to which it creates a peaceful environment has been amazing. Sometimes we just have the angle-poise lights on and the overhead ones off and it's like the reading room of a library.'

The other piece of technology of which they are particularly proud is an electronic paint-box which can do on the screen all the things an artist can do on canvas.

'Ron has scored a bullseye,' says Frank Bough. 'This is a very happy lot of people.'

141

Countdown to *Breakfast Time*. Midnight before Europe's first breakfast show is transmitted, the preparations are filmed for the archives.

1.50 am. Journalists working at their visual display units.

**4.30 am. Editor Ron Neil and Managing Editor Tony Crabb
(2nd & 4th from left) hold final production meeting.**

6.30 am, Monday 17 January 1982. Director Chris Fox in the gallery wishes *Breakfast Time* 'good luck'.

Videotape editor feeds in the first New York contribution.

Presenter Nick Ross pours a cup of coffee for Labour leader Michael Foot.

Breakfast Time press conference for Aubrey Singer, Managing Director Television, George Howard, then BBC Chairman, and Alasdair Milne, Director-General. *Below:* Champagne and red roses after a successful launch.

Below: Reporter Bob Friend sitting in his *Breakfast Time* studio in the BBC's offices at Rockefeller Center and (*above*) on screen.

Bob Friend (left) and assistant producer Tom Brook filming on Fifth Avenue.

Reporter Bob Friend sits in a small glass-sided studio on the 22nd floor of the Rockefeller Center, above New York's Fifth Avenue. Behind him a large photograph of the glittering Manhattan skyline gives an impression of cosmopolitan glamour when viewed on the screen.

He is about to record his daily five-minute news item for *Breakfast Time* which will be transmitted on the satellite at midnight and be on our 'Breakfast' screens the next morning.

This slick efficient operation belies the fact that the studio is in the middle of the open-plan offices of a former shipping company. If Friend thinks he needs a touch of make-up, then he borrows one of his female colleague's powder puffs. They rarely object.

'Make-up is entirely the department of the handbags of the staff,' says Peter Foges, producer in charge of the television department in New York. 'If you are running something as small as this you can't have such a luxury as a make-up girl.'

The BBC's New York office is on the 21st floor and by January 1982 space on the floor above had been acquired by David Webster, the BBC's Director in America, for conversion into a studio, with on-the-spot facilities for sending material back to London. The whole operation was suddenly speeded up by the Falklands crisis.

'From not having the ability to go on air either live or recorded, the capacity to edit videotape or to feed it on to a satellite from this office,' says Foges, 'our engineers produced a sort of miracle overnight. We went out shopping and over a weekend bought three VT machines and installed incoming and outgoing satellite lines. It meant that Charles Wheeler could go on the air from my desk, and be seen live nightly in the living rooms of Great Britain giving the most up-to-date information about the conflict from New York.'

The Falklands crisis emphasised the importance of having recording and editing facilities.

The next stage in what Foges calls 'the growing up of the BBC in New York' came when *Breakfast Time* Editor Ron Neil appointed Bob Friend, the BBC radio correspondent in New York, to report exclusively for his new television programme.

All this increased output takes place alongside the primary function of the New York office, which is to help producers throughout the BBC when they come to America to film complete programmes or inserts. Current affairs and sport account for half of this effort.

'After all, we are not in competition for air-time,' says Foges. 'We are a service operation for producers in that we assist in editorial contributions. In a sense we are at a producer's disposal. *Breakfast Time* is our biggest single customer but we also do pieces for *Nationwide*, *Newsnight*, sport, documentary feature programmes and the Open University.'

BBC New York has two crews, one a film crew on a rotating three-month attachment from Ealing, London and the other locally recruited. There are also three assistant producers, two researchers and a research assistant.

To meet the extra demands of *Breakfast Time*, it has been necessary for the BBC to take on two more assistant producers, another research assistant, a library clerk, research clerk and two engineers, all recruited locally.

But their target area is by no means just New York. Foges and his team must cover stories in Canada, as well as the West Coast of America, south of the border in Central America and further afield in the Caribbean.

Outside the Rockefeller Center, home of BBC New York.

Producer Peter Foges at his desk from which he sees the spire of St Patrick's Cathedral.

148

Researcher Kathy Neucom interviews rock singer Lou Reed with a two-man crew for *Entertainment USA*.

Above and below: Open University producer Charles Cooper films part of an arts course in the Museum of Modern Art with Martin Patmore, the then resident BBC Cameraman in New York.

The Living Planet

'Doing a sequel to *Life On Earth* is like being the son of a film star or following a hit record,' says Richard Brock, a producer of *Life On Earth* and the executive producer of *The Living Planet*. Both were written and presented by David Attenborough.

'Because of the great success of *Life On Earth* people will look at this one very critically,' he says. 'It broke new ground in its own way and we have to do better.'

This 12-part series has taken the Natural History Unit in Bristol three years, one million pounds and over 400 miles of film to make.

Brock's first task was to assemble a small team who could work together for such a long time. He divided the project into three sections, each responsible for four programmes. He headed one, and put producers Andrew Neal and Ned Kelly in charge of the other two. Each was backed up by an assistant producer.

'I chose Andrew because he is a very good expedition man,' says Brock, 'and Ned for his craziness in that he likes being cold and on top of mountains.'

The main BBC crew were two cameramen, Hugh Maynard and Martin Saunders, and the sound recordist Dickie Bird. Their work was supplemented by specialist freelances in different parts of the world.

Neal lived up to his reputation and led a successful expedition 100 miles into the Kalahari Desert in September 1982 to film the famous nomadic bushmen. No mean feat, as there are only about 1000 of them left roaming this desert, roughly the size of England.

But the vagaries of air travel on the African continent almost upset this ten-day trip before it had started.

151

Above: David Attenborough in zero gravity in a 707 aircraft 36,000ft above the NASA Space Center and (*left*) cameraman Martin Saunders.

Cameraman Hugh Maynard with one of the Kalahari nomads who carry their water in ostrich eggs.
Below: Attenborough with Komodo dragons in Indonesia.

Skeleton of extinct bird, the moa, in the crate which brought it from its New Zealand museum.

Skeleton *in situ*. Attenborough examining a copy of the head reproduced from the British Museum original.

The crew flew to Gaberones, the capital of Botswana, having seen their cameras and film stock safely on board. Unknown to them, the equipment was off-loaded.

'We had no alternative but to hold up the safari and pay the outfit for doing nothing while we waited,' says Neal. 'It was a nerve-wracking time. It costs just as much money to fail.'

Kelly's delay happened in December 1980 in quite a different climate at the other end of the earth. He and his crew were to be picked up in Port Stanley by the British Antarctic Survey Ship, *Bransfield*. It was to take them to the South Sandwich Islands, close to the South Pole to film penguins and seal colonies. When it was delayed, they spent Christmas there, and Kelly played snooker into the early hours with the Governor, now Sir Rex Hunt.

Kelly was getting desperate, but the ship arrived early in January and they set off to film one of the colonies of chin-strapped penguins in the Antarctic.

Landing a helicopter on tiny volcanic islands, with glaciated peaks rising sheer out of the ocean, was a formidable task. Once that had been achieved, they had to wait for the 30–40 mph winds to drop before Bird could start recording, only to discover that they had picked up the sound of the helicopter.

'We could hardly tell the Navy to clear off,' says Ned Kelly. 'After all, they had brought us there. More important, we relied on them to get us out.'

The most extraordinary experience for Attenborough and the crew was coping with weightlessness at NASA Space Center in Houston, Texas. Attenborough, television's natural history guru, was seen to levitate in a Boeing 707 aircraft at 36,000 feet and Martin Saunder's feet hardly touched the ground.

153

Freelance cameraman Neil Rettig in a Costa Rican
forest ready for a tree-top tracking shot.

Some of the 14 million chin-strapped penguins being
filmed on one of the South Sandwich Islands.

155

Match of the Day

Opposite: Match of the Day studio from the graphics desk. *Above:* Bob Wilson is wired for sound.

'Sweat and aspirins' are what gets *Match of the Day*, television's most popular football programme, on to the screen, according to its editor Bob Abrahams. Each week two games are chosen from the First Division—the BBC alternates with ITV for first choice. They are selected on knowledge of the game—recognising which matches will produce excitement, good football and, above all, goals.

'Goals and goal-mouth action, that's what people look for,' says Abrahams. He can remember only two occasions where the matches produced no goals. 'We just picked wrong that week,' he says, 'but by and large we are reasonably successful.'

Proof of this, apart from the large viewing audience, is the heavy postbag. 'We get some 100 letters a week, all of which have a point of view and we try to satisfy the majority without totally compromising our own attitudes,' says Abrahams. 'We do supportive stories about the lower division clubs.'

'Football is like a mobile bigotry in a way,' he continues. 'When the Football League started there were little village teams fighting each other in tribal conflicts. We have a good loyal audience but they always tell you what you are doing wrong. Obviously we want to show the top teams, but people always complain when their team is not shown, regardless of where it is in the League.'

Abraham sees this competitiveness as something which benefits football when it is lively and good-natured, but he abhors the violence which in recent years has sadly become a feature of the game. 'The hooliganism appals me,' he says. 'But I don't think they are football supporters, I think they use the game as a pretext.'

'You always have a crisis of conscience whether you show it or not,' says Abrahams. 'Three times out of five you try to cut it out, if it is not terribly important to show it, because it seems to produce a copy-cat effect. They have taken the rivalry too far and made it war.'

'We try to show the game at its best,' he says. 'If there are criticisms to be made, which there are, we try to meet those but there is very little knocking copy on *Match of the Day* because I don't find it helpful.'

'The referees and the linesmen are the targets for a great deal of abuse, but it seems to us when you look at the evidence of the camera they are right more times than they are wrong.'

The Football League, under the 1983 agreement, stipulates that the BBC and ITV must show every club in the First Division on their home ground once during the season. And the League will only allow each organisation to show 45 minutes from the three hours of the two matches. 'So three-quarters of the game has to come out and you leave the best in,' says Abrahams. 'The matches we show are not the games people at the ground see. It's the same content but not, for obvious reasons, the same duration.'

What Abrahams looks for from his directors is that the match be shown in a clear and informative manner. 'It is such a beautifully simple game and that's where its appeal is,' he says. 'People tend to complicate it. It is a territorial game and at one stage there was too much exciting camera-work and too many close-ups and too little information. We try to inform without instructing.'

On the Sunday Jimmy Hill and Bob Wilson arrive at Television Centre at about ten in the morning to write their scripts. Later in the day there is a 90-minute rehearsal in Studio Two just before the transmission to an audience of well over six million.

159

John Motson on the gantry, the main camera position, commenting from the monitor, holding a lip microphone.

BBC low-angle camera getting into the action.

John Motson (far left) doing the 'after match' interview, and (far right) stage manager Mike Milone.

An outside broadcast camera in the Riverside Studios.

The Decorators, a six-piece group from Ealing.

Royal Ballet dancers Sharon MacGorian and Stephen Beagley (*opposite right*), and (*above*) accompanied by The Cure.

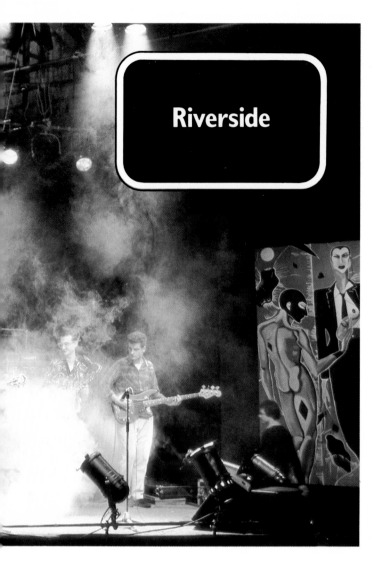

Riverside

Riverside, an alternative youth culture programme aimed at the 15–35 age group, was the brainchild of its producer, John Burrowes. One of the main reasons he wanted to do such a programme was to give air-time to up-and-coming bands and performers.

'When our first series went out in January 1982,' says Burrowes, 'this was an area which wasn't covered on television. The only groups that appeared on the screen were either in the charts or had made an album.'

As a testament to his belief that there was a lot of first-rate young talent around which was worthy of television coverage, two of those he featured on the show are now national names—Mari Wilson and Bauhaus.

But perhaps a better indication of success is that some of the existing pop shows changed their style to incorporate unknowns and at least one programme has since arrived on the screen with a similar brief. Imitation, after all, is always the sincerest form of flattery.

'If anything, there are not enough good bands to go round,' says Burrowes. 'But although we have all this competition we still get good viewing figures, around two million.'

Making the 18-part series as an outside broadcast from the Riverside Studios in Hammersmith was a fortunate choice as well. Once BBC television studios, it is now an arts centre.

'We like to feature up-and-coming artists or photographers,' says Burrowes. 'We use their work as part of the set. We also show alternative theatre, new dance groups, poets, what's happening in fashion or in the film world: anything that's likely to interest our audience. Music makes up about 25 per cent of the show.'

'We've had quite a lot of poets,' he continues. 'People like Attila the Stockbroker, Little Brother and Benjamin Zefhania, the Rasta poet. They were all very successful. They like working to an audience.'

Another feature of the show has been the audience which often included such cult figures as pop singers Boy George and Steve Strange. When the programme first started Burrowes regularly placed his presenters, who were particularly photogenic, amongst the studio viewers for them to do linking material, but more recently has has preferred to use graphics. Burrowes, his director, David G. Croft, and the programme's two researchers, Carol Fletcher and Alma Player, spend a good deal of time 'in lots of grotty pubs', as Burrowes puts it, looking for groups. Each one is seen by him before it gets on to the show.

Carol, a former dancer, is also on the look out for anything in the dance world, such as the two Royal Ballet dancers Sharon MacGorian and Stephen Beagley who performed with the band The Cure on the show.

From 6 am on the day of recording, the set and lights are made ready for the 11.30 band rehearsal.

'The first priority is getting the sound sorted out,' says Burrowes. 'We had quite a few sound problems with The Cure, who played live, because we hadn't done live music and live dance together before, but we managed to get everything sorted out.'

'You normally need between one and one and a half hours to mike-up a rock band,' he continues. 'You balance the volume of each instrument against another and then balance the vocals.'

Rehearsals for artists and presenters continue through the afternoon until seven when there is a dinner break. The audience come into the studio at 7.45 and the show is recorded from 8.30 to 9.30 and a week later it is transmitted.

Actress Coral Browne, walking across a 'Moscow' street—a salt-covered road in Dundee.

An Englishman Abroad, Alan Bennett's final play in a group of eight he has done for the BBC, is the odd one out, in much the same way that its subject, Guy Burgess, was in his Moscow exile.

'We decided to do a season of the Alan Bennett plays before Christmas 1982,' says the producer, Innes Lloyd, 'but this one had a very different style from the others, which were all in Alan Bennett territory, the North Country—literary Lowry stuff.'

The play was directed by John Schlesinger, the film director. It was his first piece for the BBC for 20 years, since the days when he was a director on *Monitor* working with his mentor, now Sir Huw Wheldon.

'I wanted enormously to do it as my return to the BBC,' says Schlesinger. 'I loved the initial script. Alan Bennett has caught all the ironies yet the loneliness of this man. I didn't envisage it on a large screen, but it's ideal for television.'

Bennett's play is based on an incident which happened to the actress Coral Browne in Moscow during the Old Vic tour in 1958 when she met Burgess, here played by Alan Bates. Drunk, he stumbled into a dressing-room and was sick in the basin. Later, he slipped Coral a note inviting her to lunch at his apartment and asking her to bring a tape-measure. It emerged he wanted her to order him some new clothes from his tailor in London.

Coral Browne told Bennett this story after she had seen his play *The Old Country* in which the central character was a traitor, living in Russia.

'I thought of her sitting in Burgess's flat listening to a Jack Buchanan record over and over again and it struck me as being incongruous,' says Bennett. 'Funny, but quite pathetic.

Politics didn't enter into it. Coral isn't a political lady. I didn't think it would make a play but a film, just an incident.'

'Burgess had no interest in the things around him in Moscow,' he continues. 'He was English to the core in the right and wrong ways. Living in Moscow must have been like being on a desert island for him, but he only had one gramophone record.'

But this bizarre tale contained another element of which Bennett was unaware when he wrote his script, naturally casting Coral Browne as herself.

'I didn't know at the time I wrote it that Coral nearly married Jack Buchanan,' he says. 'She came to within a week of marrying him. I don't know the precise details of what happened or whether he jilted her, but the song had an added poignancy for her.'

'So in the scene when she is listening to his recording of "Who Stole My Heart Away?" she is quite genuinely emotional.'

It was not possible to film in Moscow but designer Stuart Walker made a most convincing attempt at re-creating the Russian capital in Scotland.

Glasgow's City Chambers became the British Embassy and its Moss Heights council flats were used for Burgess's apartment block. Most of the other 'Moscow' filming happened in Dundee.

Fourteen workmen of the Tayside Regional Council with 80 tons of salt brought the real look of wintry Moscow to the streets of Dundee.

'We expected snow,' says the producer, Innes Lloyd, 'but the flurries that came weren't enough. At four in the morning we decided we needed the salt to be ready for an 8.30 am start.'

Director John Schlesinger (right) and cameraman Nat Crosby (far left) stalk the camera clamped to a Russian car, filming its occupants. *Below:* A 2cv is used in the filming of Alan Bates.

Dundee High School becomes a Moscow barracks. Tayside Regional Council (*below left*) spread 80 tons of salt to represent snow. *Centre:* A 'Russian' shoe shop; (*right*) banners complete the picture.

Between takes Coral Browne embroiders, Alan Bennett reflects and (*below*) Alan Bates (Guy Burgess) reads a Sunday paper.

Charles Dickson, the Special Facilities Engineer, adjusting the lighting on the macrobench.

Wildlife on One: Macrophotography

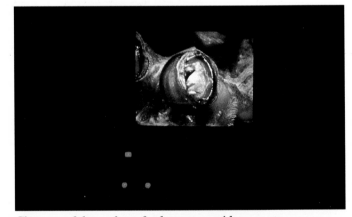

Tentacle of deep-sea squid being held
in position by clamps on the macrobench.

Close-up of the sucker of a deep-sea squid.
Below: Greater magnification shows the teeth.

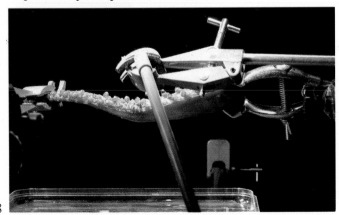

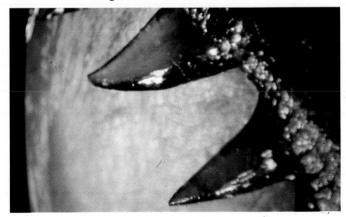

An alien from inner space with tentacles like the cratered surface of the moon and suckers with teeth.

This is not a new *Dr Who* monster created by the Visual Effects Department but how part of a deep-sea squid looks when photographed on the macrobench.

Macrophotography means up to ten-fold magnification. In practical terms this means taking bigger close-ups of smaller objects. Something like a butterfly's egg, which in real life is the size of a pin-head, can fill the television screen.

A macro object can hang in space and is a solid, while microphotography is from ten to 22-fold magnification and the specimen is flat and cellular.

The £90,000 macrophotography studio is in the basement of a house close to the BBC's Natural History Unit in Bristol. It was installed 18 months ago and is still very much in the experimental stage. It is for use on any of the BBC's programmes but its main application is natural history.

Cameramen come to the studio to learn how to adapt to a new set of controls. Charles Dickson, the Visual Facilities Engineer says: 'With these joystick controls it is more like flying helicopters or playing space invaders.'

Outside specialist units only use film but the macrophotography studio uses both film and video. The advantage of using video is that it is more sensitive and needs less light. 'One is less likely to cook the specimens,' says Dickson.

And, of course, video is easier for the cameraman to operate. A film cameraman has to squint through the eye-piece, whereas the video cameraman, working by remote controls, can sit next door and view it all on a monitor.

Videotape is also cheaper than film. A tape that can run for an hour is ideal when waiting for a butterfly's egg to hatch.

Changing magazines every ten minutes not only wastes a lot of film, but what is worse, it may mean missing the most important moment.

With video, colour can be adjusted on the spot, while film is corrected in the laboratory when the producer is not around.

The video camera used on the macrobench is an Ikegami, the same kind used for newsgathering. The camera remains still while the table rotates.

One of the problems in photographing tiny creatures or larger objects in greater detail is that with high resolution, any movement jars the image. With the camera mounted on the optical bench, the movement is cancelled out.

'You drive the camera or the bench without touching the specimen,' says the assistant producer Keenan Smart, who had put the squid under the lens. 'You can pan and tilt the camera in a very smooth, controlled fashion.'

Smart's enthusiasm for cephalopods—soft-bodied animals such as the squid, the octopus and the cuttle-fish—is boundless.

'They are the Concordes of the snail family. They are related but their relationship ends there,' he says.

'It's very, very nice to be able to demonstrate one of the squid's extraordinary tentacles by tracking down its surface over what looks like a lunar landscape and then exploring inside one of the suckers which are like craters with teeth.'

'You can do this on a macrobench,' he continues. 'My next ambition is to be able to show an incredibly small, interesting, living creature such as a bumble-bee. I would like to record a sequence which starts at the top of the bee's leg and finishes with the hook on the end.' It seems that for natural scientists, macrophotography will be the bee's knees.

Set Designer Peter Blacker in Freud's Hampstead consulting room which he recreated in the studio.
Below: Blacker and property buyer Brenda Barker measuring some of Freud's collection of antique statuettes.

Actor David Suchet researching his role. He sits at Freud's desk which was brought from Vienna.

The work of Sigmund Freud has permeated the mind of the twentieth century so thoroughly that it is virtually impossible to give a non-Freudian interpretation in any piece about the man, known as the father of psychoanalysis.

'Everyone has heard of Freud and uses the adjective but to what extent do they know him and his thinking?' says producer John Purdie. 'All they know is that Freud equals sex.'

'The Freudian legacy has become so much part of everyday behaviour and has so influenced the theatre, television and the cinema so that you can't get away from it,' he says. 'We take for granted that Woody Allen would get up and make a movie about himself, baring his soul. To ignore the existence of Freudian theory would be like living today without running water or electricity.'

Instead, he and writer Carey Harrison have made a strength of this fact.

'Carey has turned the series into a unique form of biography,' continued Purdie. 'The dying Freud analyses one last case study which is himself. This way it is not just a litany of historical incident.'

This six-hour series which took a year to research and a year to write, was something of a labour of love for Harrison. He is the son of Rex Harrison and the Viennese-born actress Lilli Palmer whose aunt, Eva Rosenfeld, was a pupil of Freud's and a respected analyst.

'We are not equipped to evaluate the work of Freud,' says Harrison. 'We are telling people about the man, which is quite a different exercise. But in telling people about him we do so in Freudian terms using his view that our patterns of behaviour stem from our early life and that the family is the biggest influence in our life. We never get very far from the womb, and in that sense our world is a very enclosed one. For this reason I think television is a marvellous medium to tell this story. Freud should be in your living room,' says Harrison. 'Television is the place for him.'

Director Moira Armstrong has emphasised this sense of introspection and confinement by having four-walled sets instead of the openness of three, as well as ceilings which are rare in television drama.

'It gives a claustrophobic feel and is closer to the reality of the space that the real location had,' says Purdie. 'It gave dramatic low-angle shots but technically the problems were quite tough. With such limited space we had to shoot on small lightweight cameras and the sound man used little "fish poles" instead of the conventional long boom mikes. This lack of room meant we didn't have such a multi-camera operation, so it became rather like shooting film which made the post-production videotape editing of major importance.'

'Instead of having four cameras which you cut between at the time of recording, you re-run sections of the scene several times and then you edit them together like film,' says Purdie. 'That's a style directors are using more and more now. This way, there is more control visually from a director's point of view, building up a scene shot by shot. In our case it was an asset because of the limited space.'

Freud came to London in 1938 as a refugee from the Nazis, and died there a year later aged 83. He lived in Maresfield Gardens, Hampstead and his study with its famous couch was a skilful copy of his study in Vienna. Both of these have now been re-created in the studio in the most meticulous detail by set designer Peter Blacker together with property buyer Brenda Barker.

Studio set: corridor in the house of Dr Joseph Breuer, Freud's patron.

Suchet studying a wedding picture of Freud and his wife Martha Bernays.

Freud (David Suchet, left) and his friend Ernst von Fleischel-Marxow (Michael Kitchen), a morphine addict, in a tepid bath to relieve the pain of withdrawal symptoms.

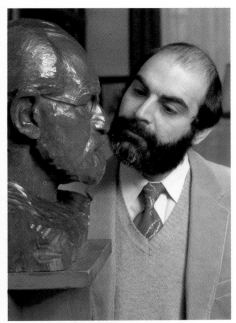

Suchet contemplating a bust of
Freud in the Hampstead house.

Suchet wearing Freud's overcoat (kept in a wardrobe in the house at Hampstead).
Overleaf: Freud bandaging von Fleischel-Marxow's gangrenous thumb.

Producer David Allen (left) and presenter Ian NcNaught-Davis demonstrating the BBC microcomputer's temperature control system.

Making the Most of the Micro

The story of the BBC microcomputer and the computer literacy project in which it was used could be called 'Making the Most of the BBC'.

'There can never have been a project where so many BBC departments have come together in one series,' says the executive producer, John Radcliffe. 'No other broadcasting organisation in the world could do this. We have the range of skills at our disposal, the educational commitment and the status in the country to get it together.'

Those at the BBC who were involved were led by the Engineering Designs Department, which was responsible for monitoring the manufacture of the computer by an outside commercial organisation; the Engineering Research Department at Kingswood Warren, for its knowledge of teletext technology; the Broadcasting Research Department, which did extensive audience surveys; two full-time education officers; the Broadcasting Support Services; BBC Enterprises and, of course, the production team.

'When we decided in the autumn of 1980 to do a television series about the principles of computing and how the microcomputer could be used,' says Radcliffe, 'there wasn't a British machine that matched up to our ideas of what was needed in a personal computer. The ones around didn't have the range of facilities we thought necessary, and they were very expensive. After a good deal of thought it was decided to produce a new machine as the BBC microcomputer.'

This was based on a specification drawn up by BBC engineers after much discussion within the BBC, as well as with

176

The microcomputer in the gallery is seen producing some of the credits used in the programme.

The microcomputer with its display monitor and disc drive which is the computer's memory store.

Ian Trackman, series' software consultant, programming the microcomputer for the BBC buggy to get out of a maze.

people in education and government.

The series and the computer were separate operations, the computer being seen as an accompaniment to the series.

What no one predicted was the massive immediate response to the computer, even before the first series had gone out in January 1982. A fifth, *Computer Town* is now in preparation.

As a result, the computer, and the two series, *The Computer Programme* and *Making the Most of the Micro*, in their various forms, have netted the BBC over £1 million in revenue.

More than seven million people watched at least one programme in the first series; by spring 1983, 80,000 books had been sold.

Britain has over half a million personal computers, the highest number per head of population in the world. This domestic revolution has only taken place in the last 12 months and the BBC can rightly claim to have been a major force in it.

'We were lucky to have launched our project as early as we did,' says Radcliffe, 'because it has come at exactly the right time. As a result we are fortunate to have a world lead in television programmes about computer literacy.'

It has been estimated that one small home computer is equivalent to the computer power available to a large multi-national company 15 years ago.

'You can sit at your kitchen table and use it for fun or make it as complex as you want,' says Robin Mudge, one of the directors on *Making the Most of the Micro*. 'We are limited only by our imagination.'

177

'Mediaeval village' being added to an existing archway.

Frank Finlay (Witchsmeller Pursuivant) and Robert East (Prince Harry).

178

'If there had been a television service in the fifteenth century,' says producer John Lloyd, 'and you had done a contemporary situation comedy, what would it have been like?'

After the huge success of *Not the Nine O'Clock News*, Lloyd and one of its stars, Rowan Atkinson, pondered what they should do next.

'We were sick to death of jokes about Shirley Williams not being able to comb her hair,' says Lloyd, 'so we said why don't we do a mediaeval sitcom with lots of wonderful filming, marvellous period faces, and with strange, peculiar costumes? It's an area not really touched on in television so we decided to do a big costume drama, but intentionally funny.'

A small, hitherto unheard-of tome came to their rescue. It was called *The Tragedy of the Black Adder*.

'It was such a feeble story, so unimportant and inconsequential, like the Hitler Diaries,' says Lloyd. 'In fact, it *was* the Hitler Diaries of the fifteenth century, that no one took any notice of.'

The book was written by Prince Edmund, Duke of Edinburgh—the part played by Atkinson.

Rowan Atkinson (Edmund, Duke of Edinburgh) keeping the rain off his 'bald' head between takes.

Atkinson 'engulfed' in flames which were some feet away, half-way between him and the camera.

'He was an extremely unpleasant little man who accidentally murdered his uncle Richard III at the Battle of Bosworth,' says Lloyd. 'Of course, he is nothing like the present Duke of Edinburgh, apart from the hair-cut.'

A sense of period was essential, and designer Chris Hull, make-up artist Deanne Turner and costume designer Odile Dicks-Mireaux all went to great lengths to make it as authentic as possible. For example, fruit and vegetables like tomatoes and potatoes do not appear because they did not exist in England at the time.

'We were blessed by a wonderfully creative team,' says Lloyd. 'They tackled the series as if it were an award-winning drama serial.'

'We wanted to get away from the kind of thing Mel Brooks did in *History of the World—Part One* which is the film I hate most of all,' says Lloyd. 'He had perfectly ordinary people wearing funny costumes, making jokes like "why don't we use the telephone, oh, we can't, it hasn't been invented yet". There was no need for us to go over the top because the clothes of the period were so extraordinary and looked so ludicrous. For

example, Rowan has a pair of shoes—his best—which were two-feet long and very pointy with a gold chain from the tip of the toe to a garter around the knee. We got that from a history book I had at school.'

Much of the filming was done at Alnwick Castle, principal seat of the Dukes of Northumberland. To an existing archway in the middle of a field, they built a 70-foot-long run of a mediaeval village.

In front of this, Edmund was to be burnt at the stake for alleged witchcraft, in the company of another wrong-doer, Balderic (Tony Robinson). There was no danger that the actors would get singed. A fire was lit between them and the camera. On film it looked as if they were being engulfed by smoke and flames but they were in fact some feet away. The only hazard for them was getting rain on their bald heads.

Back in the studio, Peter Cook was playing Richard III as a very cross, headless ghost. Cook was decapitated by a painless electronic device called colour separation overlay (CSO) whereby the camera keys out anything in blue. So Cook went blue in the face in order to lose his head.

179

Camera rehearsal for the Palm Sunday programme from Norwich Cathedral.

Songs of Praise

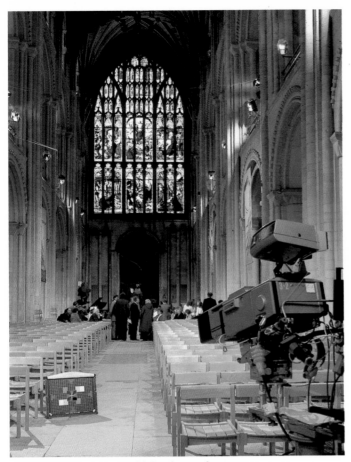

Lining up the camera, which takes an hour.

Congregations from Norwich churches gather to rehearse.

'There's always one person in the choir who saves himself for the night and then gives his all,' says producer Jim Murray. 'He usually sings out of tune and cracked, but the choir is big enough so nobody watching would notice the difference.'

Songs of Praise, now in its 22nd year, is one of the BBC's hardy annuals which goes out weekly for nine months of the year, each programme drawing an average audience of ten and a half million, a healthy number by anyone's standards.

'Programmes like this are part of the furniture,' says Murray. 'We deliver the goods week after week and have to get variety into what appears to be a format. We endeavour to keep it as fresh as possible without making it so fresh that people don't like it.'

'*Songs of Praise* is a television programme about the Christian life of a community, reflected through the eyes of some of the members of that community who talk about their faith or their lives,' says Murray. 'That community comes together to sing songs, most of which have been chosen by the people interviewed. It is not a transmission of a church service.'

The reason the church is always full of people is because the congregation is made up from churches of all denominations in the area. There has also been a Christian/Jewish programme, and another was of Hindi hymns.

'We are well to the fore in practical ecumenicalism,' says Murray. 'We never say, "this week it is Roman Catholic or Church of England".'

To ensure an overall musical standard, a choir is created from the combined choirs of all the churches taking part. They are not robed and they often make up about one-third of the congregation.

Michael Armitage, vicar of St John's Angell Town in Brixton, is musical adviser to the programme.

'We try generally to raise the standard of hymn singing and introduce some new ones,' says Jim Murray. 'But naturally people like the old favourites which for variety's sake we can do in a slightly different manner, say, with a folk group.'

The programme is always recorded in stereo, although heard in mono on television. This is because of the great demand for the *Songs of Praise* record.

The programme visits churches by invitation, except on special occasions, such as Remembrance Day, when the producer may make the first approach.

Once a church has invited the BBC, a leaflet is sent out explaining what is involved. A broadcast will take two weekdays, one for rehearsal. The amount of disruption to the life of a church depends on its size. Rigging for television can take up to a week, the exception being when the programme came from Durham Cathedral it took three!

In Norwich Cathedral the engineers and technicians were there for a week installing 120 lamps and half a mile of cable, stringing the stereo microphones high above the central aisle and setting up the cameras.

The programme visits churches throughout the British Isles and recently it went international. The *Songs of Praise* team were the first non-news crew to go to the Falklands.

They have also been to Cyprus and Germany.

The team's background is not necessarily in religion. 'While it's important to know the difference between the Bible and Mrs Beeton's cookery book we don't need to be theologians to survive,' says Murray. 'We're making television programmes, not church services.'

181

Overleaf: 120 lamps and half a mile
of lighting cable illuminate Norwich Cathedral.

Local school children rehearse one of the two programmes recorded at Norwich Cathedral.

Before the recording, the organist conducts the choir and congregation from the pulpit.
Below: Five choir boys sing a special item for the programme.

One of the Open University's two modern control rooms.
Below: Lighting equipment in one of the two new studios.

In many ways, the relationship between the BBC and the Open University is like a good marriage. The two are formally joined together in a legal partnership without time limit for the production and transmission of television and radio programmes, yet they remain entirely independent bodies.

'We are fully a part of the Corporation—like the External Services,' says Robert Rowland, Head of BBC's Open University Production Centre. 'We, like them, are differently financed. Our money comes from the Department of Education and Science, not from the licence fee.'

In 1983 the budget for the Open University Production Centre was £10 million, one-sixth of the overall budget for the Open University. In one year they produce around 250 television programmes (18 per cent of which were for video cassette in 1983), and 400 sound programmes (80 per cent being audio cassettes in 1983).

Since September 1981, the BBC Open University Production Centre has been based on the campus of the Open University at Milton Keynes, 50 miles north of London.

Its first home was at Alexandra Palace which in 1969 had just been vacated by BBC News.

There are about 400 full-time BBC personnel who work in production, engineering, television design, graphic design and film services. Sixty producers cover the six faculties of Arts, Educational Studies, Social Sciences, Science, Technology and Mathematics.

'They are recruited for their academic quality so they can contribute fully to academic discussions,' says Robert Rowland. 'If this were not the case the partnership would not be so well balanced and creative. We choose people of high academic skill with particular expertise and train them to

Professor Colin Rourke recording a third level mathematics course at the Open University, Milton Keynes.

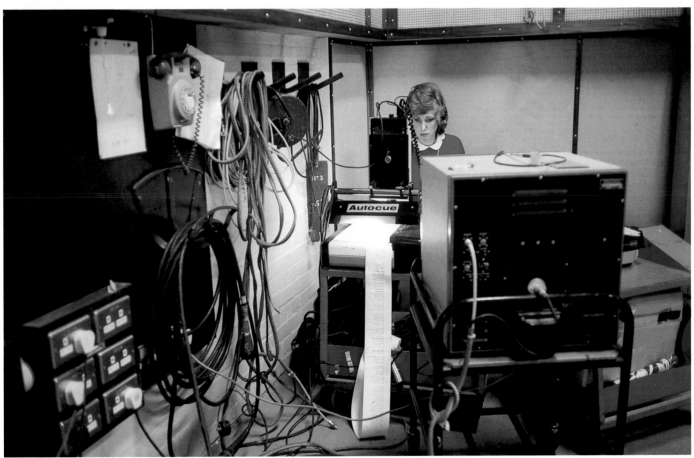

Autocue, a method of projecting the script in front of the camera lens, is used in a high
percentage of OU programmes, especially science. It aids continuity and keeping to time.

The OU's Visual Effects workshop makes anything from life-size pterodactyls to (*below*) perspex models.

Mathematics producer Jack Koumi with make-up assistant Lynda Burr and Visual Effects assistant Christine Bestavachvili, discussing props for a third level higher-mathematics course.

become producers.' Unlike other BBC producers, they work in both audio and visual media because many of the courses combine the two.

The BBC studio complex at Milton Keynes is purpose built and one of the most up to date. There are two television studios, two sound studios, film editing, dubbing and review areas, film and video rostrum cameras, videotape recording and editing facilities, telecine equipment, a microscopy unit for science and technology programmes, electronic and mechanical maintenance areas and outside broadcast capability. There are also scenic, graphic and visual effects, design and production areas, a scenery workshop and stores, photographic, costume and make-up areas.

The Production Gallery, Vision, Lighting and Sound Control rooms for TV Studio 1 contain modern vision mixing, sound mixing, tape and disc facilities and micro-chip based lighting control.

Television can excite and invigorate the learning process. Mathematical concepts, for example, can be vividly illustrated by imaginative graphics and visual effects. The range of output is very wide, but though the audience's purposes are precise, Robert Rowland believes that the production values and quality should be as high as any other part of the BBC.

He believes that one of the greatest impacts on Open University learning in the future could be the video cassette and the video disc. In 1982 it was discovered that 42 per cent of students had easy access to a video cassette recorder, and this figure is increasing all the time.

'We predicted the video cassette revolution correctly and we're adapting to meet this development, but broadcasting will remain central to the University's openness,' he says.

A complicated theorem in the third level mathematics course is illustrated by sculpted fibre-glass models.

189

An invited audience enjoy the traditional music of Ossian, the Irish folk group, playing Celtic instruments.

As I Roved Out

'When we move out, the sheep and cows move in,' says producer Tony McAuley, referring to the large barn-like hall owned by the Royal Ulster Agricultural Society where he records his six-part folk music series *As I Roved Out*.

The hall is needed from March until the beginning of June by the Society for shows and exhibitions. So BBC Belfast have to vacate the outside broadcast studio they have set up there. It has been used by them as a 'temporary' measure for the last 14 years.

'It takes us three weeks to dismantle everything,' he says. 'When we've taken down the lights and stored away the

Ossian in the Royal Ulster Agricultural Society grounds.

scenery it looks just like a furniture warehouse. And, of course, when we return we have to put everything up again and that takes another three weeks.'

McAuley started his series in 1976 as a showcase for Irish folk music. It proved so popular that it has become an annual event.

'We have a living tradition of folk music in Ireland,' says McAuley, 'and the quality of our folk music is reckoned to be the best in the world.'

Despite the title, the programme does not normally rove out on location, although McAuley hopes this will change in the future. However, on one memorable occasion they did take to the road and recorded a programme in Antrim in the spring.

'The cameramen were rigged up like Arctic explorers while the artists were miming to songs in a howling gale trying to look as if they were having a good time,' he says. 'It was ridiculous.'

The RUAS hall may lack many things, but warmth both in terms of the studio and the audience, is not one of them.

'It has a good atmosphere to work in,' says McAuley, 'it's not got that antiseptic feel studios often have. We have developed a growing affection for it over the years.'

Northern Ireland's regional output is between six and a half to seven hours a week, of which half is news and current affairs. They supply 30 network programmes a year apart from news reports. There are 650 permanent staff with 200 on short-term employment with the BBC.

'We are the smallest of the three national regions,' says James Hawthorne, Controller of Northern Ireland, 'but measured in other ways, we are one of the largest. Northern Ireland has been *the* place in terms of news coverage for the last 14 years. Generally speaking, the Belfast Newsroom has very close links with the London operation if a big story is happening. Our chaps are used to having the lead story in the news bulletins and for this reason we have a rather good news animal in Northern Ireland.'

In 1983, a major development scheme was completed. This now provides specially built news and current affairs studios and replaces a 45-year-old television studio once used for radio.

191

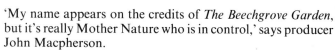
Assistant producer David Gloag starts the identification clock.

The Beechgrove Garden

'My name appears on the credits of *The Beechgrove Garden*, but it's really Mother Nature who is in control,' says producer John Macpherson.

The Beechgrove Garden had its first series in 1978 and was created purely for gardeners in Scotland where it is produced and shown.

'Prior to this, most gardening programmes on television were made in the south of England', says John Macpherson. 'The weather conditions and the soil are considerably different there so the advice given was not relevant to Scotland. As Aberdeen is half-way up Scotland we can justifiably claim to serve the whole country.'

The Beechgrove Garden is very much a working garden and failure plays as important a part as success. Certainly Macpherson and his crew do not claim to be first-class

gardeners, like the presenters Jim McColl and George Barron, who are professional gardeners.

'They are gardeners first and presenters next,' says Macpherson. 'I keep my address secret because I am ashamed of my own garden. It's fair to say the production team are not gardeners, otherwise we could become dreadfully self-indulgent.'

Like all television producers, Macpherson plans ahead. He does this, however, in the full knowledge that his plans may be undermined by a plague of greenfly or an unexpected burst of sunshine which may bring a rank of flowers into bloom ahead of time.

'When these things happen we tear up one item and do another,' he says. 'It's a programme where we are showing the real conditions and we want to let it reflect exactly what

Aerial view of the Beechgrove Garden with raised flower beds for the disabled in the foreground.

happens to our garden. Not everything we grow succeeds. Some things die. When this occurs we try and explain why.'

'People soon see that we are not a glossy magazine type of programme,' says Macpherson. 'I think they enjoy it because of that, especially if they succeed where we fail.'

The garden itself is in the back yard of BBC Broadcasting House in Aberdeen. It was once a wilderness of a few scrubby trees and rough grass, overlooked by a 110-foot-tall mast. The trees and the grass have gone, replaced by a fruit-house full of apple and peach trees, vines and strawberries, a vegetable plot, heather beds, herbaceous borders, a cold frame area, a garden adapted for the disabled and a potting shed. The mast, however, remains.

'A necessary evil,' is what John Macpherson calls it. 'It is the first hop in the microwave link to Broadcasting House in Glasgow,' he says. 'We have no videotape recordings, so when the programme is put together it is beamed up that mast and sent to Glasgow to be recorded.'

Macpherson and his team have endeavoured to make it serve a horticultural purpose as well. They have planted a clematis—that attractive, multi-flowered, rapid-growth climber which they hope one day will draw attention away from what he calls an 'eyesore'.

The mast, which is never shown in any of the programmes, puts another constraint on the production team.

'It has a large shadow,' says Macpherson, 'so when it's sunny our items have to be done before midday otherwise the whole of the lawn would be covered with lattice-work shadow.'

'Of course, sometimes it does rain in Aberdeen.'

193

Part of the 110-ft-high transmission mast. Its horticultural interest lies in the clematis at its base.

Alex Hodgson, resident gardener, spring cleaning the patio pond.

195

The model railway garden with (left to right)
Jim McColl, George Barron and producer John Macpherson.

OB Unit recording (*above and below*) in the Maternity Wing of the Glangwili Hospital, Carmarthen.

BBC Wales's longest running and most popular soap opera *Pobol y Cwm* (*People of the Valley*) can now no longer be seen on the BBC.

It goes out on Channel Four Wales as part of the ten hours which BBC Wales contributes to the Welsh language channel, known as S4C. This came into being in November 1982 and is also supplied with material from the local independent station, HTV. Channel Four Wales is a unique partnership between the BBC and ITV for which there is no equivalent anywhere else in Great Britain.

In preparation for the launch of S4C, the BBC increased the number of episodes from 26 to 35 a year.

Pobol y Cwm started in 1974 and was the idea of John Hefin, the BBC's Head of Drama in Wales.

'The series has all the elements you would expect to find in a typical Welsh village,' says producer Gwyn Hughes Jones who was a floor manager on the series when it started. 'The village shop, with its talkative, gossipy shop-keeper Maggie the Post (Harriet Lewis), the local garage, the pub and an old people's home, where another favourite character called Harri Parri (Charles Williams) works as the gardener.'

Hughes Jones has discovered that it also has a great appeal for those learning Welsh, and for people living in the anglicised areas of Wales who have an infinity with the language. The popularity of *Pobol y Cwm* has been partly responsible for the success of the fourth channel in Wales. At times it has an audience of 240,000 which is well over half the Welsh-speaking population, and it is consistently one of the top-rating programmes on Channel Four.

Apart from increasing their output, the biggest production change was doing the first series for S4C with their own outside broadcast unit.

In the spring of 1982, BBC Wales got a 'new' two-camera unit.

'Well, it wasn't exactly new,' says Hughes Jones, 'but it was new to us. It was an old Open University scanner which we now use to do drama.'

'It enabled us to increase our outside work and to get closer to the areas in which the village should be based. We don't say exactly where we are, we exist in the imagination of our viewers, wherever they like to place us. But people generally tend to locate us around Carmarthen.'

If this brought a greater sense of reality to the series on the screen, it also brought reality a little too close while on location.

'At times it was very difficult to carry on with the recording because the response in the street was incredible,' says Hughes Jones. 'People regard the characters with warmth and when they see them they want to chat to them, like old friends.'

'On one occasion we were recording a fight sequence in Carmarthen market,' he continues, 'and two gentlemen came out of the crowd and tried to stop the two actors from acting.'

The production of *Pobol y Cwm* is a joint effort all along the way. Ideas for 35 episodes come from five teams, each of which have two people known as story-liners. The story-lines are then discussed with the producer and the script editors. From this a detailed synopsis of each episode emerges. These are then sent to the dozen authors who work on the series.

'I think each year we gain in strength,' says Hughes Jones. 'We are now working from a firm base with a lot of experience behind us. With that professional know-how it is a good environment to bring new writers, actors and production people into this "family" of ours. We tend to be like that on this series.'

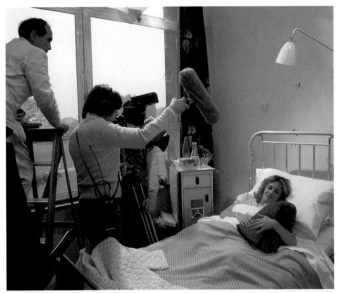

Gillian Thomas (Sabrina) rehearses motherhood with an anorak.

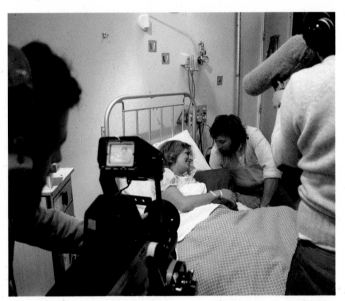

Dafydd Hywl (husband Jack) arrives, and (*below*) so does baby.

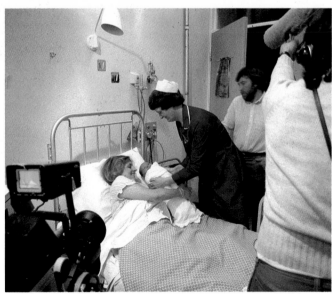

Overleaf: Next day, the OB unit recording in a farmyard.

197

Inside the Sanatan Deeva Mandal Hindu temple in Bristol, which also serves as a community centre.

Asian Magazine

Outside the temple, director Waseem Mahmood with cameraman
John Kenway and sound recordist John Parker.

Asian Magazine crew in the Hindu temple reporting on its conversion from a Christian church.

When the Asian Unit came into being in 1965, its primary function was to provide information about this country to make life easier for the many newly arrived Asians.

'The word used then was integration,' says Ashok Rampal, executive producer. 'Now it is multi-cultural and multi-racial. For the sake of living together as one community the programme can't stay a one-way process.'

'We want to impart information aimed at the white population about what it is to be Asian. This way it is hoped that both sides know a little about each other and some good may come from that.'

Another way in which the programme has inevitably changed is that there is now a second generation, and even a third, who are Asian in origin but totally British by birth and education.

'We try and encourage parents to understand the position the younger generation find themselves in,' says Rampal. 'They have chosen to bring their children here, and these are being brought up in the environment of this country. They are not the children of small villages back home in India, Pakistan or Bangladesh. Equally, we put it to the younger generation that they should try and see their parents' view.'

The Asian Unit is based at the BBC's Pebble Mill studios in Birmingham and provides both television and radio coverage. This includes a half-hour television magazine programme on Sunday mornings on BBC1, for 52 weeks of the year. There is also a half-hour radio programme on Radio 4 on Sunday mornings.

The nine people working in the Unit include, apart from Rampal, four assistant producers, two production assistants and two secretaries. They cover both television and radio.

London, Manchester and Glasgow are the main areas for most of their stories, although as assistant producer Krishan Gould says: 'We will go anywhere for an interesting story.' He gives the example of an Indian who lives in Glasgow and makes an annual trip to the Hebridean island of Barra to sell clothes to the locals.

The television programmes are usually in English or Hindi or Urdu and, Rampal says, reach over 80 per cent of the Asian population. Location work is all on film, never video, and it makes up 40 per cent of the programme, the rest being studio based.

The policy of the unit is not to become involved in controversial racial issues. If there are race riots they will report them as a news item but they do not comment or analyse the event, believing there is room for that in other programmes.

'We aim at five-minute items in our programmes,' says Rampal. 'These include lighter pieces on music or dance, some straightforward information, say, about a relevant government bill and something about an activity in the local community.'

'But equally we are trying to reflect the changes in our viewers,' continues Rampal. 'We can't sweep the more difficult problems under the carpet, we must show what is happening in society.'

One of the most provocative reports has been about runaway girls.

'We got an overwhelming reaction from that with a tremendous number of complaints,' says Rampal. 'But it happens and if we talk about it there's a chance somebody will do something.'

201

Samantha Pym dancing at Sanatan Deeva Mandal temple watched by women visitors.

Saranjit 'Sammy' Birdi, a 23-year-old architecture student in Bristol, who is also an accomplished poet and disco dancer, rehearsing in a discotheque.

Broadcasting House, Newcastle, once a lying-in hospital.

BBC North East and Cumbria

Mike Neville, *Look North* presenter, in the Newcastle studio.

Eric Robson completes a documentary on political reporting.

BBC camera crew standing on a table to film the declaration.

Broadcasting House in Newcastle was once a lying-in hospital. John Frost, the Regional Television Manager, thinks it is more like a destroyer these days. 'There is no space wasted,' he says. 'Every cupboard has something in it.'

The staff squeeze into the L-shaped 900 square-foot studio. This space is a tenth the size of Studio One at Television Centre which is 9000 square feet.

Newcastle, one of eight BBC regional stations, produces 205 programme hours a year of which 70 are features, the rest being mainly news and current affairs.

'Many national programmes are made in the North East, but ours have a local viewpoint which producers who live and work here can uniquely contribute', says Frost. 'They serve to make life in our region better known and understood by the nation as a whole.'

In three years' time BBC Newcastle will vacate their cosy, Georgian home and move into one of the most advanced electronic studios in Europe. It is being built on the two-and-a-half-acre Fenham Barracks site at a cost of eight million pounds. The new centre will also house Radio Newcastle bringing radio and television under one roof.

'Building this new complex is a mark of the BBC's confidence in regional broadcasting,' says Frost.

Newcastle's main function is catering for the region. This covers six counties and runs from the east coast to the west coast, north to Berwick and south to Yorkshire. Once the cradle of industry, they are currently [1983] feeling unemployment of between 22 and 30 per cent. Television plays a major role in their lives both as entertainment and, we hope, as a link towards the fuller enjoyment of life.

'People in the North-East watch two and a half hours more

television winter and summer than anywhere else in the country,' says Frost.

One of the most popular programmes is the daily magazine *Look North* which is presented by Mike Neville, a Geordie, who has become something of a folk hero in the 18 years he has been with the show.

A regional station provides rich opportunity for learning how to cope with those terrible moments when the screen goes blank, something which happens with much less frequency in the network centres.

'Mike has won a reputation for having the appropriate phrase when, say, a film machine breaks down,' says Frost. 'As there is only one machine, it can happen without warning.'

Most of Newcastle's output is on film, except for studio-based pieces. But for ten weeks of the year, this most northerly television station in England has the use of an outside broadcast unit which is shared between Manchester, Leeds and Cumbria.

'There is a great yearning for the countryside, particularly in the industrial areas,' says Frost, 'and one of our three feature producers does a series of programmes called *North Country* with this OB unit.'

Newcastle's main programme thrust is for local consumption, although a number of their productions are shown on the network over the year. However, in spring 1983 during the Darlington by-election, the station found itself the centre not just for BBC crews from London but for the rest of the world as well.

Perhaps the experience could best be summed up by the title of the half-hour feature Eric Robson made about the by-election. It was called *The Three Weeks the Circus Hit Town.* 205

The Mayor of Darlington gives the by-election result.

Candidate Screaming Lord Sutch who placed a bet on the number
of votes he would poll, collects his winnings (*right*).

A vox pop in the streets of Darlington. A voter tells *Look North* reporter Tony Baker what he thought of the result.

John Humphrys has last minute discussion with his editor John Anderson.

In the News Studio, two of four remote controlled cameras.

The Newsroom on the sixth floor of Television Centre during one of the editorial conferences.

Preparation for the *Nine O'Clock News* begins early in the morning but, of course, any item can be jettisoned at a moment's notice if a major story breaks shortly before transmission, or even after nine.

Of all live BBC broadcasts news programmes are the most unpredictable, but unpredictability is the essence of news broadcasting.

'One seldom goes into a programme with a set of stories which remains constant,' says John Humphrys, main presenter of the *Nine O'Clock News*. 'New scripts are coming in all the time while we are on the air. There have been times when a big story happened four minutes into the News and we turned the whole bulletin round there and then.'

Humphrys has been in this job for two years. His appointment marked a radical change in the style of BBC newscasting. Peter Woon, Editor of Television News, wanted journalists as presenters rather than the old style newsreaders who had little involvement in writing the news scripts.

Humphrys spent six years in the United States for the BBC during the Watergate period, and followed this with three years as their Southern African correspondent. After nearly a decade away from Britain, he became the BBC's London-based Diplomatic Correspondent, and 12 months later he was made a presenter of the *Nine O'Clock News*.

He writes the introductions to many of the stories he reads, and brings his journalistic experience to their presentation. He is in by 10.30 each working morning and does not leave until close to midnight after he has read the late news on BBC1.

His first duty is discussing with the editor of the day and his deputy what stories will form part of the *Nine O'Clock News*. Each of the three news bulletins has its own editorial team.

Humphrys could be involved in doing an interview or a report in the field, but usually he works in tandem with the newsroom writers, and the reporters.

The object of the exercise is for him to be as familiar with as many as possible of the 15 or so stories which make up an average night's News.

At three in the afternoon, there is a meeting to agree the basic shape of the programme in the large open-plan Newsroom on the sixth floor of Television Centre. It is attended by Humphrys, the editor of the day, his deputy, the writers and news producers and some of the technical staff.

At 3.50 there is a small meeting in Woon's office to keep him informed of the content of the bulletin and another immediately following the 5.40 News, 'to put the finishing touches to the running order'.

'In the main, editorial decisions are made by the editor of the day,' says Humphrys. 'It is unusual for Peter Woon to change anything. These conferences are designed to inform him rather than seek his approval but obviously he has the ultimate responsibility.'

At 8.30 Humphrys makes his way to the small, recently refurbished news studio N1 on the sixth floor to face four remote control cameras and an Autocue. This is paced to the speed of his delivery and has about three words to the line with each line taking a second to read. Usually, only half the stories are on Autocue by the time the programme goes on the air because of the constant updating.

'If at the end of the News the audience have forgotten who read it but have remembered what were the main items, I think we have succeeded,' John Humphrys says. 'I don't like the notion that news presenters become personalities.'

Peter Woon, Editor, Television News (far left), is advised of the running order of the evening bulletin by editor of the day, John Anderson (2nd left).

John Humphrys looking through videotape footage to enable him to write his introduction to the story.

Humphrys altering his script and the Autocue tape.

Captions for the *Nine O'Clock News* being lined up.

Humphrys rehearses his lead story.

Macheath (Roger Daltry) and Polly Peachum (Carol Hall).

The Beggar's Opera

Mrs Peachum (Patricia Routledge) with Peachum (Stratford Johns).

'One of the things about working with Jonathan Miller,' says Dennis Channon, technical manager and lighting director, 'is that generally we have in mind the work of a well-known artist. It is particularly helpful if you are doing a stylised production because then you know exactly what is in the producer's mind.'

There is a rich heritage when it comes to *The Beggar's Opera*. William Hogarth illustrated many scenes from John Gay's ballad opera, including perhaps the most famous, Macheath, the highwayman, in Newgate Prison.

'With the scene in the prison I wanted to create a claustrophobic atmosphere,' he says. 'The best results are produced by the smallest number of lights, isolating the people, confining them in small areas.'

'Looking at a painting gives you ideas about colours,' says Channon. 'With this production I decided to light with very little colour. I wanted the lights to have a slightly old-masterish look so I used a very light amber filter. When you put this on the lights it gives an impression of the varnished, warm look of a painting.'

The reverse of this technique is the Western, says Channon, where the colours are very exaggerated and the lights strong and bold. The story is straightforward and unsubtle, and the lighting reflects this.

'With Shakespeare or opera you do more muted lighting,' says Channon, 'anything more would become obtrusive and unnecessary.'

'The colours you use are blue and amber,' he continues. 'You can't see a warm colour without having a cold colour to balance it. You must have the contrast because the eye adjusts to that.'

'Jonathan wanted this production to be in the style of Hogarth but also to be slightly Brechtian,' says Channon. 'In other words, to capture the atmosphere of the time while always reminding the audience that it is a studio production; going half-way towards eighteenth-century reality and then showing it to be artificial.'

'On the other hand, you do have to give the actors an environment in which they can do their best,' he continues. 'This is the reason I always spend a lot of time at the rehearsals. It is important to know where an actor is standing as I do fairly localised light sources. Also, it's a good way of getting to know the actors. Then it becomes something we all do together.'

From the moment Dennis Channon reads the script he is building up a total picture which will eventually evolve into his lighting plot. The script will tell him the mood of the play, the time of day, the season of the year and whether it is studio-based or to be filmed/recorded on location.

The next stage is a planning meeting with Jonathan Miller, the set designer, make-up artist, costume designer and sound supervisors. The designer will have a floor plan and sketches of the scenery and any lighting effects will be discussed. If it is a complicated production there will be more than one planning meeting.

'This process is purely the mechanics of collecting information,' says Channon. 'Then slowly I go through the camera script, scene by scene, visualising where the actors are in conjunction with the camera shots.'

The night before the recording, studio lighting is positioned from information on the lighting plot. When Channon arrives in the morning he begins the complicated process of fine setting each lamp to be ready for the camera rehearsal, and ultimately for the recording.

A portrait of Polly Peachum.

Producer/director Jonathan Miller on the set with cameraman from crew 7, Andy Hallam.

213

Scenes of Hogarthian London were painted on heavy gauze and hung behind the set.

Make-up artist Eileen Mair working with Roger Daltry and Carol Hall.

Jonathan Miller giving notes to Carol Hall while she has her hair tidied before a take.

David Myerscough-Jones's heavily timbered set is a montage of eighteenth-century London.

The open-sided set enabled the camera to record from any angle.

The Boat Race

A final practice row for Oxford on the morning of the boat race.

The rules say that the Boat Race between Oxford and Cambridge Universities must be held in the Easter break. It has got to start two hours before the top of the tide at London Bridge and must be rowed on the flow so that the tide is with the crews from Putney to Mortlake. This gives them the fastest water to row.

Thus, the event is a movable feast and could occur as late as 5.30 pm. In 1983 the 129th Boat Race took place at five. Twenty minutes later Oxford, in dark blue, made it their eighth year in succession to triumph over their rivals in light blue, Cambridge.

Covering the four and a half miles along the Thames is one of the BBC's most complicated outside broadcast operations. Cameras are placed along the bank, there is one in a helicopter and another on a launch on the river.

Campbell Ferguson, the assistant producer, says: 'The production team are very much in the hands of their technical colleagues. None of it would happen without the detailed technical planning of Roy Carpenter, the senior field engineer, and Sam Branter, the engineering manager.'

'You can do the start and finish of the race with cameras cabled back to OB vans but the bit in between is by radio links, transmitting the signals to the main site at Putney.'

Maintaining these links is vital because in his small hut, Harry Carpenter, the commentator, only sees the beginning of the 20-minute race as a live event. The rest he views on monitors.

Ferguson and John Philips, the producer, spend eight hours walking up and down the Thames six weeks before the race, plotting the camera positions for the best television shots.

There are 15 altogether, including the one in the helicopter,

the one on the boat, the *Pembroke Puffin*, which follows the race, and at the finish, a hand-held camera is used on a coaching launch close to the Ibis boathouse.

What makes it such a major technical exercise is the fact that all the cameras along the river are operated by remote control. This means that engineers sitting in their outside broadcast vans some miles away at the main site are constantly adjusting the technical quality of the picture, allowing the cameraman to get on with his job of recording the event.

The *Pembroke Puffin* has a camera mounted onto it. It is also loaded with radio link equipment and a mobile generator. This transmitting equipment on the boat sends the pictures to a number of receiving sites along the river.

A rehearsal before the event indicates at which points the producer must switch to the next camera on the route to maintain the clarity of the picture.

It is at such moments that the producer may decide to screen pictures from the helicopter which has also been fitted with a transmitter to send back its output to the OB site at Ashlone Road, Putney.

'The biggest improvement in 1983 was the fact that we used a helicopter with a special mounting which keeps the camera rock solid,' says Ferguson. 'It gives the best pictures possible. The other innovation was a water level hand-held camera at Mortlake at the end of the race.'

'We wanted to get reaction shots,' says Ferguson. 'But we weren't happy with the result mainly because a Port of London Authority boat came between us and the crews. There's not too much you can do about that. But we will improve on the coverage next time. It's an ever improving cycle. We look to the future.'

217

Cameraman Frank Hudson carries his ENG camera aboard a launch for close-up personality shots at the finish. *Below:* Moments after the Oxford victory.

Hugs and prizes for the winners, (*below*) hugs and consolation for the losers.

Restoration lunch for *All the World's a Stage*.

The vast army of the BBC, like its military equivalent, marches on its stomach, whether that 'march' is a trip to one of the nine tea bars at Television Centre or a sit down meal in a tent at Wimbledon.

BBC catering can mean anything from a humble cup of tea — 20,000 are consumed in a week at the Centre — to smoked salmon and beef Wellington on the Sixth Floor when the top executives are entertaining important guests.

Leslie Abell, executive chef of Television Centre says: 'These days the "in" food is yogourt. Soups and sausages have been hammered over the last ten years.'

Every major outside broadcast has a portable kitchen attached to it complete with stoves, refrigerators and freezers. At Aintree, in fact, there were two — one near the main site and the other beside Bechers Brook.

When actors are rehearsing, they and their producers, eat in the top-floor restaurant of what has been dubbed the 'Acton Hilton' above the seven floors of rehearsal rooms. They can have anything from a roll to roast beef and Yorkshire pudding, with wine if they wish.

Meal-break but no *Summer Wine* for the cast and crew.

Aintree: the not-so-*Grand National* dining room . . .
and the temporary BBC kitchen.

Nigel Hawthorne, Peter Whitmore, Derek Fowlds and Paul Eddington take tea at the Acton 'Hilton'.

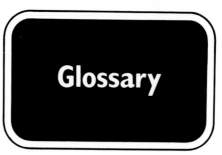

Glossary

Animation bench: Apparatus used in making cartoon or animated films by photographing a number of drawings, usually frame by frame with a Rostrum camera.

Autocue: A device mounted on a camera so that an artist/contributor can read the script while looking at the lens.

Backcloth: A scene painted on canvas to form the background to action.

Boom: A telescopic arm for positioning a microphone.

Camera Crane: A mobile camera mounting with a jib arm which can be raised and lowered, rotating around its fulcrum.

Camera Script: Script marked up with shot numbers, cutting points, camera, lighting, sound directions.

Cherry Picker: Mobile hoist. Form of camera tower used on OBs for heights from 40′ to 150′.

Clapper Board: Board used for scene and take numbering and cueing in sound filming.

Colour Roving Eye (CRE): An estate car modified to take a camera channel so that the camera can be mounted on the roof or on a mounting adjacent to the vehicle. It can feed into a standard OB unit by radio transmitting its picture back, provided it is within line of sight of the receiving point.

Colour Separation Overlay (CSO): By shooting a scene against a background of a pre-determined colour, an electronic switch will enable another source to be overlaid into the background or to infill foreground.

Dubbing: The action of recording and by extension the preparation of a composite sound track from several ingredients such as commentary, music, dialogue and effects, all recorded on separate tracks laid for dubbing.

Equaliser: An apparatus designed to compensate for attenuation distortion or phase distortion introduced by lines or equipment.

Footage: Length of film expressed in feet. Collection of related films sequences e.g. Stock Footage.

Fringing: The appearance of spurious edges of incorrect colour at the margins of coloured areas.

Jib: The arm of a camera crane.

Lip microphone: A specially designed microphone held close to the speaker's mouth when exclusion of ambient sound is necessary e.g. for sport commentators.

Magazine: Container for film in camera and projector.

Mole Crane: 3-man-operated camera mounting with counter-balanced jib arm.

OB: Outside broadcast.

Pilot: Programme made as a sample of a possible series.

Propagation: Transmission of electro-magnetic waves from radio and television transmittors to the home receiver.

Radio Link: Radio circuit. Used for sound and/or vision.

Rostrum Camera: Camera and mounting used to film static objects, e.g. pictures, maps with controlled zoom, and tracking and panning for frame to frame shooting.

Scanner: Name given to a mobile control room.

Scenery Flat: A completely flat piece of scenery made in different widths and heights.

Technical Run: Run through of complete production at outside rehearsal specifically for the technicians responsible for lighting, sound, cameras etc.

Telecine: An apparatus for generating television pictures from motion picture film.

Test Card: Caption specially designed to convey the full range of monochrome and colour information for lining-up receivers.

Vision Mixer: Vision mixers work in the studio control room and are responsible to the Producer/Director for selection of sources by cutting, mixing, fading, etc according to the picture sequence or narrative.

VT: Video Tape

Zoom: Lens with a continuously variable angle of view over a defined range, e.g. 5 - 50 .